CRITICAL INSIGHTS INTO THE NOVELS OF P.OHINTON MISTRY

CRITICAL INSIGHTS INTO THE NOVELS OF ROHINTON MISTRY

By

Dr. Sujata Chakravorty

Associate Professor & Head
Department of English
Dayanand Arya Kanya Mahavidyalaya
Nagpur (India)

DPH

DISCOVERY PUBLISHING HOUSE PVT. LTD.
NEW DELHI-110 002

Published by:

Tilak Wasan

DISCOVERY PUBLISHING HOUSE PVT. LTD.
4383/4B, Ansari Road, Darya Ganj
New Delhi-110 002 (India)
Phone : +91-11-23279245, 43596064-65
Fax : +91-11-23253475
E-mail : discoverypublishinghouse@gmail.com
sales@discoverypublishinggroup.com
parul.wasan@gmail.com
web : www.discoverypublishinggroup.com

First Edition: **2014**

ISBN: 978-93-5056-510-0

Critical Insights into the Novels of Rohinton Mistry

Printed at:
Dynamic Printers
Delhi

DEDICATION

THIS BOOK IS DEDICATED TO MY FAMILY

Preface

Indo-English literature today has come centre-stage and has occupied a very important place in the literary world courtesy novelists like Salman Rushdie, Shobha De, Amitava Ghosh, Vikram Seth. Also included in this category are sparkling names like Ved Mehta, Bharati Mukherjee. Preceding them are gems like Mulk Raj Anand, Nirad C. Chowdhary, R.K. Narayan, Raja Rao, Khushwant Singh, Shashti Brata, etc. Indo-English literature is a global phenomenon today; it has in effect globalized the literary movement and impacted the whole world of literature immeasurably.

Neither imagination, nor displacement, not even Diaspora affected these writer's beliefs and conviction in the areas of politics, society, custom, culture, fanaticism, fundamentalism, etc. Literature is an exposition of culture and conviction; it unites and does not divide. It helps spread amity and communication across the international boundary. It is prudent at this stage to place Rohinton Mistry's work against the back-drop of Indo-English literature.

In the case of Rohinton Mistry it is portrayal of angst, ecstasy, and anguish of Parsi community settled in India. Rohinton Mistry, himself a Parsi had obvious involvement in matters Parsi. He is a descendant of the Parsi Diaspora. His fore-fathers had migrated from Iran to India decades back and accepted things Indian excepting religion and religious rites.

This book, entitled, ***'Critical Insights into the Novels of Rohinton Mistry'*** examines the novels of Mistry with respect to the Parsi Environment in India, his complete absorption with the city of Bombay, various factors that constitute a family and attempts to unravel Mistry's attitude towards women in general.

–Sujata Chakravorty

Contents

1

The World of Rohinton Mistry

The evaluation and analysis of a writer's work necessitates an honest effort at understanding the possible factors that have gone into making him what he is at present. This chapter aims at examining closely aspects of the life, work and milieu which helped Rohinton Mistry blossom into a writer par excellence.

Rohinton Mistry's birth in 1952, in Bombay, was most opportune as it allowed him glimpses into the most happening city of India, post Independence. He spent a full 23 years in India, before immigrating to Canada in 1975. His formative years, spent in Bombay, the city of his birth, allowed him to register the various goings-on in all possible fields that he cared to note sub-consciously. These sub-conscious registrations find place in his detailed representation of the city he knew too well in its various moods, and hues.

Mistry's parents, Behram Mistry and Freny Jhaveri Misty brought up four children, three sons and a daughter. Rohinton Mistry, born on 3rd July, 1952, was the middle son of the three, his sister being younger to him. Cyrus Mistry the play wright and short story writer is his younger brother. His father worked in the field of advertising, while his mother, the home-maker,

> "Was happy in that role doing the miracle that all mothers perform of making what was barely enough seem like abundance. We didn't have new clothes and shoes as often as we might have liked but were certainly better off than half the population".[1]

Mistry attended two of the best schools in Bombay – first the Villa Theresa Primary School, and then St. Xavier's High School which only proves his statement further. He also did not live in the kind of Parsi housing estate that he describes meticulously, yet powerfully in three of his published works of fiction – "Firozsha Baag' in *Tales from Firozsha Baag*, 'Khodadad Building' in *Such A Long Journey* and 'Chateau Felicity in *Family Matters*.

He later graduated from the St. Xavier's College in Bombay in the year 1974 with Mathematics and Economics as subjects. The subjects were not of his choice, however, and he had to study them as boys in those days in India were generally expected to take up a course in Science and not Arts degrees. As Mistry has said in an interview,

> "The B.Sc. was the lowest thing expected. The more Ambitions fellows became engineers and doctors, and so, lacking in ambition, I chose the lowest thing of what was expected'.[2]

In the same college, he met Freny Elavia, the woman he later married. She graduated an year earlier than him, as she concentrated on studies only.

Mistry, however, managed to grow his hair long as against the accepted norm of the day – executing a rebellion of sorts and played his guitar in clubs as the self-styled 'Bob Dylan of Bombay.'[3] When he was about 14 years of age, he was mesmerized by an older family friend's singing and playing the guitar. He was given some basic tips by the same friend and so proceeded to play the harmonica. He acquired a guitar by disposing of an old violin that belonged to the family. He was completely self- taught in this newly acquired hobby. Bob Dylan was his idol – 'Mr. Tambourine Man', 'Blowing in the Wind',

'The Times they are A-Changing' were some of his favourite. He tried writing a few songs himself, but does not hold his efforts in high, esteem, merely remarking, 'It was more trying to be like Bob Dylan than to express anything original'.[4]

When he was about 19 years of age, in the year 1971, he took part in an open air concert, 100 miles outside of Bombay. Thousands of kids enjoyed themselves for three days with India's rock bands playing music of well known groups such as Rolling Stoves, Jethro Tull, the Moody Blues, etc. Mistry performed for the crowd, guitar in hand, singing folk songs. Occasionally he played in clubs and restaurants and college functions and rock concerts. At that time he seriously considered a career as a folk singer. His effort in singing bore fruit in the year 1975, with Polydor releasing an EP, Ronnie Mistry, on which he song his own compositions and traditional folk songs.

Mistry had already graduated in the year 1974. It was time to take another, conscious decision – That of immigrating to a foreign country. It was the general expectation, from family and society alike, that a young man must travel west wards in search of greener pastures. 'Australia was racist, America was not too inviting with Vietnam and all that rubbish, and England wasn't England any more. Freny Elavia had relatives in Canada and. she decided to emigrate there after her graduation in 1974. Mistry decided to follow her there in 1975 and they subsequently got married that same year. The year 1975 therefore became quite significant in Mistry's life as it proved to be one in which major decisions of his life were taken. In answer to a question of interviewer Adil Jussawalla in 1988, when he was on a visit to Bombay after a gap of 13 years, he says in this context 'I wanted to be famous in the music world there. I wanted to be a star'.[5] His aspirations to 'be as star' in the world of music, however, was nipped in the bud as the music teacher in the school he joined in Toronto did not rate him highly. The teacher's remark, 'You're already as good as someone. Who's been playing for six months'[6] dampened his spirits considerably and spelt an end to his career in music.

Rohinton Mistry had to struggle in the first years of his arrival in Brampton, a suburb of Toronto. He applied for jobs in many places, but was surprised to find that his degree in Maths and Economics were not of much help. Fortunately, his wife, Freny, already had a job there first as a secretary and then school teacher. When he put in his application at McDonald's, he was asked to shave off his beard, if he was serious about the job. Mistry had no choice but to agree, but wasn't offered the job ultimately. Soon after, he was offered a position as a clerk in the accounting department of the Canadian Imperial Bank of Commerce. He worked for about ten years in the bank from 1975 to 1985, working his way up from a clerk to supervisor of the customer-service department.

While working at the bank, Mistry, wasn't very satisfied and realized that his true calling lay elsewhere. In 1978, he along with his wife enrolled for some evening courses at York University, subsequently transferring to the University of Toronto. The bank at which he was working subsidized the course for him. He opted for English Literature and Philosophy – subjects he was interested in since his college days at Bombay, way back in 1971. Apart from his busy office schedule, he managed time to read for his classes on the subway, steal time off from his lunch hour at the bank, in the E.J.Pratt library or Roberts library before class. The course introduced him to writers like Chekov, Malamud, Turgenev, Hawthorne, Trollop, Eliot, Bellow's *Humboldt's Gift*, Thackeray's *Vanity Fair*, Melville's *Moby Dick* and poets like Whitman and Frost. The three year course ensured him second bachelor's degree in 1982, at Woods Worth College. So, impressed was Mistry with the writers he studied, that he said to his wife, 'wouldn't' it be nice, to be a writer?[7]

On another occasion, he admitted to interviewer Veena Gokhale, 'I set myself this dream of trying to write like these people, this wonderful stuff'.[8] The seeds of his true vocation were sown in his mind and soon opportunity struck at his door, in the form of an advertisement in the fall of 1982, in *The Varsity* announcing the first Hart House Literary Contest. His wife inspired him to participate and try out his literary skills. Mistry took her seriously, entered the competition, won the first prize and thus embarked upon a literary career which is bedecked with jewels all the way.

But the fact of his being a writer was again subject to chance. He was not too happy in his bank job, so he and his wife took some evening classes at the University of Toronto. And this time he ensured that the subjects were to his liking – English Literature and Philosophy. He was much impressed and influenced by the wide gamut of great writers the course introduced him to. The seeds of desire to be able to write like these writers formed in his mind and soon destiny smiled upon him – he took part in the Hart House competition and got first prize for his story 'One Sunday'. His success story and dream run of awards did not stop with that – and it must be mentioned here that he has won a prize for almost all of his published work.

Mention must also be made of his younger brother, Cyrus Mistry, who had already decided to become a writer and won the sultan Padamsee Prize for his play Doongaji House. It was Cyrus who introduced Mistry to the rich world of books for the first time when they lived together in Bombay. It was Cyrus again who made him realize later that 'Bombay is as viable a city for fiction'[9] and that it was not necessary to write about New York or Paris in order to be an acclaimed writer. So it is Bombay that Mistry writes about – the city of his birth and the place where he grew up and which occupies such an important place in his consciousness that he can't seem to stop writing about it. Apart from a couple of stories in Tales from Firozsha Baay which are set in Canada, it is Bombay as locale for Mistry so far as Wessex is for Hardy and Dublin for Joyce. When Mistry had won several awards and was in the full glare of media publicity, it was Cyrus who came to his rescue once again by lending him a copy of Cyril Connolly's *The Enemies of Promise* – which reiterated Mistry's belief of staying aloof from the media and concentrating on his writing.[10]

Rohinton Mistry took a conscious decision to emigrate to Canada from Bombay in 1975. By this time he had already completed his Bachelor of Science degree in Mathematics and Economics. He was also a singer of sorts and had made a name for himself in the local music scene. In Toronto his aspirations for a career in music was nipped in the bud. Meanwhile he joined the Canadian Imperial Bank of Commerce as a clerk and accountant, and worked there for ten years. Simultaneously, he along with wife Freny, took up evening classes at the University of Toronto, studying for a B.A. in English and Philosophy. His entering and subsequently winning the first Hart House Literary Contest of the University of Toronto in 1983, with the short story 'One Sunday', set the ball of his literary career rolling.

Very soon, he published a collection of his short stories, entitled *Tales from Firozsha Baag* (1987), which was followed by his first novel, *Such a Long Journey* (1991), second novel, *A Fine Balance* (1995) and his third novel *Family Matters* (2002). There are a few common threads running though his fiction – the country of his birth forming the background to his works, prominently being one. Till date he has set only two of his short stories in Canada. To often asked questions that want to know when he will write about Canada, he answers.

> "I prefer to write about that which engages my imagination. At the present time that is India. It's very naïve to assume that you leave a place and you go to a new country and you start a new life and it's a new chapter – it's not. Canada is the middle of the book. At some point you have to write the beginning."[11].

Mistry's straying into the Indo-English literary area heralded the arrival of a colossus, gentle, polished, sophisticated and humane. Indo-English literary world shall forever remain indebted and beholden to this giant amongst Indian writers in English language. Over a period of time Mistry carved out a niche for his writings in the areas of Indo -English literature and established himself as unrivalled. Rohinton Mistry is the subject of this book. The following chapters reveal exhaustively Mistry, his personality, his writings, his philosophy, his conviction and his faith and belief and in effect Mistry in totality, a wholesome human being.

Rohinton Mistry's creative writing skills got recognized way back in the year 1963 when he was about eleven years of age studying in the fifth standard. He was given a creative writing assignment by his school teacher. He thought it to be a good idea to write a story about a cricket bat in the first person. He let his imagination run free with the idea. He became a willow tree in Kashmir who's chopped down and made into a cricket bat, and subsequently sent to a sporting goods store in Bombay. The cricket bat is eventually bought by a man for his son to play with. The boy uses him to play cricket with his friends and the story ends on that note. This autobiography of a cricket bat was immensely appreciated by the teacher and also finds a place in the annual school magazine. But, Mistry says, 'that's as far as my literary efforts went'.[12] He did not follow up his success with other such endeavours. He did not fancy a career in creative writing either. Some years later, he taught himself to play the guitar after getting a few basic tips from an older family friend. He idolized the North American Singer Bob Dylan and aspired to be like him. He even accompanied himself with the harmonica and guitar, like Dylan. It was about this time that he penned some songs inspired by Dylan's greatest hit albums. But Mistry did not hold his compositions in high esteem, quickly dismissing it with 'It was very derivative – about love, and the used adolescent nonsense's [13]. Nevertheless, he sang these songs, along with some others for an EP, released by Polydor, entitled Ronnie Mistry in 1975.

Apart from these forays in the world of creative writing, there was nothing serious from Mistry's pen for many years to come. He emigrated to Canada in 1975, got married to Freny Elavia in the same year and some months later got a job as a clerk in the accounting department of the Canadian Imperial

Bank of Commerce. Not fully satisfied with only his bank job, he along with wife took up some evening classes at first York University and later University of Toronto. The classes in English Literature and Philosophy stimulated his appetite. He enjoyed reading the poets Whitman and Frost, and novelists Eliot, Trollope, Hawthorne, Thackeray, Bellow, Melville, etc. He reads voraciously all the while and again feels something amiss, not blissfully happy with his bank job either. He feels it within that this job is just like a station on the way to his true vocation which is something else. Increasingly he feels a burning desire to be able to write like the great masters he has been reading lately.

Mistry does not have to wait long to try his talents though. His wife soon brings to his notice an advertisement in the Varsity in the fall of 1982, anouncing the first Hart House Literary Contest. She encourages him to participate. He has now to find time in which to accomplish this feat. He tackles the problem easily though – with the help of a small white lie. He claims to be sick on the Thursday and Friday before the weekend off. Thus having gained four days at his disposal, he settles down to write for about six to seven hours a day, producing the first draft of 'One Sunday'. He thoroughly enjoyed the experience, 'That was the first time I'd ever sat ever sat down to write, and I think I was fascinated by the process it self – watching the words appear at the typewriter[14]. The story is about a young boy's realization that smashing a human being's head is quite different from killing a rat with his cricket bat. In total disgust at his past behaviour, he breaks his beloved bat.

Mistry entered the Hart House Competition with the story – 'One Sunday'. The panel of judges, headed by poet Dorothy Livesay adjudged it to be the best. Considerably encouraged by the outcome, and pleasantly surprised, he kept on writing and again entered the same competition the next year. His story this time was 'Lend me Your Light'. The story which begins with an epigraph from Tagore's Gitanjali, deals with the theme of immigration of two boys, Jamshed to the US and Kersi to

Cannada and the latter's brother Percy makes a conscious choice to stay on in India. When Kersi comes for a short visit back, he finds India to be worsethan what he had left behind. He knows and realizes Percy's stand to be right, but does not have the guts to make a conscious choice to stay on in India. The short story writer, Mavis Gallant is at the head of the July. She too awards him the first prize and makes a special note to editors John Metcalf and Leon Rooke to keep him in mind for their forthcoming anthology of short stories. Mistry did win the Hart House prize for two consecutive years, but his dream of 'a cash prize with the added incentive of seeing your story bound in leather', could not be fulfilled as the sponsors were facing a financial crunch. This is interestingly reminiscent of his yet to be published "A Fine Balance – "everything ends badly" – Maneck Kohlah's words ring true here.

Mistry's dream run of awards, however, continued. The next year, 1985 saw his story 'Auspicious Occasion' being published in The News press Anthology: Best Canadian Short Fiction and receiving the contributor's award for it. The chain of awards resulted in publishers lining up outside his door, all interested in publishing his first anthology as soon as he was ready for it. He finally gave the nod to Penguin Canada who published his Tales from Firozsha Baag in 1987. Penguin England retained the rights to bring out the book in UK and Commonwealth. Houghton Muffing published the book in the USA with the title Swimming Lessons and other stories from Firozsha Baag. This book was shortlisted for the Canadian Governor General's Award.

Before being published in the form of an anthology, all except one of the short stories were published in some of the top literary magazines in Canada. Tales from Firozsha Baag are a collection of short stories, set in a Parsi Housing estate Firozsha Baag in Bombay. The stories are all inter-connected and present a realistic picture of life in its true colours. As has already been mentioned, Mistry did not live in one such housing estate, but some of his friends did, which provided him with enough opportunity to form impressions. As admitted to Ali Lakhani in an interview, India and Bombay in particular, continue to engage his imagination. Therefore he writes about things he knows best – reconstructs from memory and paints it with imagination.

Rohinton Mistry does not openly acknowledge any influences on his work. It is left to the readers and critics at large to gauge what could be some possible ones on his mind and consequently reflected in his work. Here it might be argued that a person's birth and growing up in a certain environment all contribute towards the shaping of his/her imagination. The position the family enjoys in society, the mindset it has, the values it inculcates in the children, the religion it follows – and the rigidity with which religious and other customs are practiced – all contribute towards marking the individual into what he/she is.

In the case of Mistry it is known that he was born in Bombay in 1952, roughly about five years after India became independent. He was the second child in his family – there being a brother elder to him and another one and a sister younger to him. He had a relatively happy childhood, with his parents taking very good care of the children to the best of their ability. He was sent to two of the best schools in Bombay – education in the formative years goes a long way in making or marring a person's life. In college he was again influenced by the general expectations from family and society that a boy must either go in for studies in the field of engineering or medicine or at least an 'ordinary' degree in Science – B.Sc. Here he took advantage of the existing loopholes in the curriculum and opted for Maths and Economics so that he did not have to attend practice classes that other science subjects required.

Besides these, Mistry was much impressed by an older family friend's playing the guitar at a get together and getting some basic tips from him, he taught himself to play – a la Bob Dylan style. He was even impressed enough to write a few songs like his idol. Occasionally he performed at clubs, restaurants, college functions and rock concerts. He also had grown his hair long – a sign of rebellion to societal norms. His emigration to Cananda in 1975 can also be looked upon as an influence of the times – people who wanted to make it big, had to travel west wards.

One major influence on Mistry was that of his being born in a Parsi family. The Parsis, as is known had come to India from Iran where they were being persecuted by the Muslim rulers. They had sought refuge in Gujarat, where the then ruler, Jadhav Rana had put conditions to their stay – which had all been agreed upon. They agreed to speak the Gujarati language, give up arms and their women had to adopt Indian costumes. These and other conditions imposed meant that they had to change their way of life forever. The Parsis in India are thus in Diaspora – all Parsi sensibility is informed and influenced by this memory. After the independence of India, the Parsis again experienced a sense of insecurity – in that they were closer to the British colonizers and felt that for this they would be oppressed by the Hindu fanatics. Some Parsis therefore migrated westwards in search of greener pastures – to Australia, the USA, the UK and Canada. It is to the last of these places that Mistry chose as a possible place of residence. It must be noted here, that this was willingly done by people of the Parsi community. The Parsis living outside India therefore are in double Diaspora. Mistry's writing is to a great extent influenced by this sense of double displacement.

But the fact of his being a writer was again subject to chance. He was not too happy in his bank job, so he and his wife took some evening classes at the University of Toronto. And this time he ensured that the subjects were to his liking – English Literature and Philosophy. He was much impressed and influenced by the wide gamut of great writers the course pointed him to the seeds of desire to be able to write like these writers formed in his mind and soon destiny smiled upon him – he took part in the Hart House competition and got first prize for his story 'One Sunday'. His success story and dream run of awards did not stop with that – and it must be mentioned here that he has won a prize for almost all of his published work.

Mention must also be made of his younger brother, Cyrus Mistry, who had already decided to become a writer and won the sultan Padamsee Prize for his play Doongaji House. It was Cyrus who introduced Mistry to the rich world of books for the first time when they lived together in Bombay. It was Cyrus again who made him realize later that 'Bombay is as viable a city for fiction' and that it was not necessary to write about New York or Paris in order to be an acclaimed writer. So it is Bombay that Mistry writes about – The city of his birth and the place where he grew up and which occupies such an important place in his consciousness that he can't seem to stop writing about it. Apart from a couple of stories in Tales from Firozsha Baag which are set in Canada, it is Bombay as locale for Mistry so far as Wessex is for Hardy and Dublin for Joyce. When Mistry had won several awards and was in the full glare of media publicity, it was Cyrus who came to his rescue once again by lending him a copy of Cyril Connoully's The Enemies of Promise – which reiterated Mistry's belief of staying aloof from the media and concentrating on his writing.[18]

REFERENCES

1. Angela Lambert, 'Touched with Fire', *The Guardian,* April 26, 2002.
2. Stacey Gibson, 'Such a Long Journey', *University of Toronto Magazine*, Summer 2002.
3. John Bemrose, 'Salaam Bombay: Rohinton Mistry Again Recreates his Birthplace', Maclean's April 22, 2002.
4. Stacey Gibson,' Such a Long Journey', *University of Toronto Magazine*, Summer 2002.
5. Adil Jussawalla, 'Writers Aren't Self-Centred', Midday, September 9, 1998.
6. *Ibid*.
7. Val Ross, *Globe and Mail,* November 30, 1991, p. 9, Quoted in Amritjit Singh, "Rohinton Mistry (1952-)", *Writers of the Indian Diaspora*: *A Bio-Bibliographical Critical Source.* Nelson Emmanuel S(Ed.) Connecticut: Green wood Press, 1993. pp. 207-218.

8. Stacey Gibson.
9. Indu Saraiya, 'Luck Played a Great Part', T*he Independent,* August 4, 1991.
10. Adil Jussawalla.
11. Veena Gokhale, 'How Memory Lives and Dies', *The Sunday Review*, The Times of India, October 227, 1996.
12. Stacey Gibson, 'Such a Long Journey', *University of Toronto Magazine,* Summer 2002.
13. *Ibid.*
14. *Ibid.*
15. Adil Jussawalla, 'Writers Aren't Self-Centred', *Midday,* September 9, 1988.
16. Indu Saraiya, 'Luck Played a Great Part', T*he Independent,* August 4, 1991.
17. Adil Jussawalla, 'Writers Aren't Self-Centred', *Midday,* September 9, 1988.
18. Adil jussawala, 'Writers Aren't Self–Centred', *Midday*, September 9, 1988.

2

Parsiness in Rohinton Mistry's Novels

The fictional work of Rohinton Mistry can be located in diverse disciplines simultaneously – diasporic reality, Indian post coloniality and Parsi history. These fields allow the reader to probe the multilayered meanings offered in his fiction – as Mistry does not deliberate upon them himself. He prefers to leave it to the world of critics, reviewers and academics to identify the possible themes and issues in his fiction. In the published works of Mistry till date, I have identified four themes to be largely recurrent – the Parsi Environment in India, Bombay as background, Matters of the family, and Discordant feminine voices.

Parsi writers have, over the years, made their presence felt in the Indian English writing scenario. They were among the first Indian communities to have willingly accepted education in the English language. This was subsequently followed by their creativity in the field of Indian English Literature with Behram Malabari, Cornelia Sorabji, Fredoon Kabarji, A.F. Khabardar, C.S. Nazir, D.M. Wadia, P.P. Mehrjee and D.F. Karaka Jr. publishing short stories, novels, poems, sketches and plays. However, in these Parsi writers belonging to the late eighteenth and early nineteenth centuries, there is not much assertion on Parsipanu (the Gujarati word for Parsiness).

It is only in the works of post-Independence Parsi writers like Dina Mehta, Bapsi Sidhwa, Firdaus Kanga, Farrukh Dhondy, Boman Desai and Rohinton Mistry that an 'ethnic atrophy'[1] syndrome is clearly detected. Firdaus Kanga in *Trying to Grow*, Rohinton Mistry in *Tales from Firzosha Baag* and *Such A Long Journey*, Farrukh Dhondy in *Bombay Duck* and Bapsi Sidhwa in *The Crow Eaters* and *The Pakistani Bride* demonstrate their writers' extreme sensitivity to the various insecurities and anxieties felt by their community.

These writers are actively and consciously engaged not only in carving out a niche for themselves as a distinct community but also asserting the uniqueness of their community through the very effective medium of their fiction. Nilufer Bharucha in her essay 'Why All this Parsiness' addresses some very pertinent questions to this phenomenon and also goes on to answer them satisfactorily. At first she traces the arrival of the Parsis in India from the turbulent times in Iran (then Persia) when it was invaded by the Arab rulers. Fearing a forced conversion to Islam, they fled from Iran and arrived in Sanjan, Gujarat, India. They were given refuge and granted permission to stay on provided they acceded to certain conditions. The conditions required them to lay down weapons, not proselytize, give up their language, costumes and customs in favour of those of the rulers and not inter-marry with the local population. For faithfully adhering to these conditions, they retained the right to practice their monotheistic religion – Zoroastrianism. The Parsis, however, developed uneasy feelings towards their rulers, being left with no other choice.

Gradually the Parsis settled down in their adopted land taking avid interest in life around them and furthering their prospects – they became agriculturists, artisans and traders, living mainly in and around the coastal areas of Gujarat. Subsequent European invasions saw the Parsis acting as middlemen for the rulers. With the British coming to power in 1770, the Parsis made Bombay their stronghold and are concentrated there in majority more than any other place ever since. The Parsis were also greatly impressed by the lifestyle of the British and emulated them in manners, customs and costumes. They greatly identified with the colonizers and became very westernized which in turn increased the animosity of the Indian mainstream towards their community.

With the independence of India, the Parsis were again in a position which many would not be envious of. They felt increasingly marginalized and threatened by the dominant Hindu Community. Some of them who could not adjust to the changed circumstances preferred to try their luck westwards. The people of the community who stayed back – not wanting to a relocate again, are however, very small in number –

"The Parsis are a minuscule minority in India and number only 80,000 today."[2]

Various factors like late marriages, low birth rate, high rate of divorce, children of Parsi females who married outside the community not accepted into the faith, etc. have contributed to the ever declining numbers. Nilufer Bharucha asserts,

> "It is in such a life and death situation that the Parsis are making their last grand stand asserting their glorious Persian past, their Indian connection and their new Western experiences. All these aspects are reflected in the assertion of Parsi identity in recent fiction written by them"[3]

This chapter traces the Parsi history from the time the Parsis reached India seeking shelter. It is a well known fact that they agreed to mix with the local population of Gujarat and not proselytize. Mistry like other members of his community is worried about the diminishing number of Parsis in India and the world. His novels record not only the history of the Parsis before their arrival in India, but also faithfully record their rich cultural heritage, customs, religious practices, their Towers of Silence, Cuisine and their idiosyncrasies. Mistry has gone on record to say that after the glorious past of the Parsis, people should remember them by these literary works if not anything else.

In Family Matters, Inspector Masalavala, Jal and Dr. Fitter discuss this very problem.

> "Just before you came, Jal," said Inspector Masalawala, "we were chatting about the future of the Parsi community."... "Vultures and crematoriums both will be redundant," declared Dr. Fitter, "If there are no Parsis to feed them. What's your opinion?"... "We've been a small community right from the beginning. But we've survived, and prospered."... "Those were different times, a different world," said Inspector Masalavala, not in a mood to tolerate optimism. "The experts are confident that fifty years hence, there will be no Parsis left." [FM - 412].

Neither imagination nor displacement nor even diaspora affected the Parsi writer's beliefs and conviction in the areas of politics, society, custom, culture, fanaticism, fundamentalism, etc. Literature is an exposition of culture and conviction; it unites and does not divide. It helps spread amity and communication across the international boundary. Any literary attempt by a Parsi is beset with Parsi affairs and afflictions; and this is because of self imposed restrictions in the delicate and sensitive areas of marriage, succession, last rites, etc.

The community's diaspora from Iran to India and his migration to Canada has not dented his faith – he continues to be on the rails. Rohinton is found to be ruthlessly objective on his comments on Parsi society. His format is fictional but statements are factual; that is precisely where Rohinton stands out amongst the migrant writers.

Industrious Parsis have indulged in all areas of industrial and trading activities with vengeance and with perfection scaling ever newer heights, thus blazing a new path for others to tread upon. Parsis even though number wise a minority community have been creating wealth for others to reap a handsome harvest. This is a dual contribution towards generation of national wealth. Rohinton Mistry has been especially brilliant in putting forth this area of Parsi endeavour.

Everything English attracted the Parsis most - English Education, English Dress code, English Social Courtesies and Etiquettes, all of these had impact on Mistry and hence on his writings. Let us not forget that Mistry was born much after India achieved independence, to be precise in the year 1952. Even then things English had profound influence on him. As a matter of fact, Indo English literature started acquiring the status of a world phenomenon after independence; Mistry is a by product of this movement.

Rohinton Mistry is not enigmatic in his approach; he is direct and forthright in his expressions; that is why he is so objective about Parsi community residing in India. His settlement in Canada has not dimmed his views on India and Indians; is he patriotic? Of course yes. That is where he scores over a non-resident Indo English writer like Bharati Mukherjee who opines 'I could have been a greater success if I had stuck to Indian themes. But I don't think one can live in America and still write about an India that has changed while one has been away?'

Sasthi Brata while making the following comment on Bharati Mukherjee indirectly praises Rohinton Mistry for his stand,'Coarse, ignorant, insensitive and thoroughly despicable'.

Rohinton Mistry was not appreciative of not realizing the importance of things Indian while staying far away from the homeland. Distance from the country of origin did not have any devastating effect on the psyche of Mistry as against few others. Rohinton Mistry has been a phenomenal success. Mistry regrets but does not despair; he is faithful with a positive bent of mind. His approach is constructive and proceeds smoothly with his unflinching conviction. Mistry does not gloat in exuberance of immigration. On the contrary he has made a conscious effort white staying abroad to remain Indian, cultivate Indian culture and write profusely on India and Indians.

Rohinton Mistry is a Zoroastrian Parsi who migrated to Canada in 1975. He thus has an insider's knowledge of his community's glorious past in Iran; their subsequent forced flight to India in order to safeguard their religious interests; their willing submission to the conditions imposed by Jadav Rana; their adapting to the Indian way of life and speaking the local language (Gujarati); their near total identification with the British colonizers; the resultant feel of unease and insecurity in an Independent India; the final conscious choice to move towards the west in search of greener pastures culminating in a second Diaspora for their community. His writing stands testimony to his community's trials and tribulations through the ages and is informed by the success stories of the few who have made it to the top in various fields and the vast majority of those who are relatively unknown and barely manage to eke out a living. These are the people focused upon in his fictional work.

The first story in the collection, 'Auspicious Occasion' was first published in Canadian Fiction and bagged the contributor's award. The story deals extensively with Parsi Customs, manners, rituals, their particular use of language and the constant reminder of being a marginalized community, pitted against the 'other' dominant, majority community. Mistry makes no attempt to glamorize their life style, but portrays them as ordinary, middle class persons, who face the same problems as any other community does in India – problems of irregular water- supply, peeling paint and falling plaster in the monsoon season and leaking W.C.S. the story's main characters, Rustomji and Mehroo, twenty years apart in age had got married when he was thirty-six, and she merely sixteen. At fifty years, he had taken to wearing dentures. Mehroo, in the prime of her youth was an orthodox Parsi and observed the important dates on the Parsi Calender with the accompanying rituals. The story centers around the auspicious occasion of Behram Roje – how the couple want it to be perfect but things start going wrong first thing in the morning with the WC from the flat upstairs leaking on Rustomji's head. After a bath and clean white clothes, on his way to the fire temple, he is spat on by someone chewing paan, this ruining his day completely. Mehroo too returns from the fire temple, much agonised over the murder of revered priest – Dustoor Dhunjisha. Even after their plans for the morning had gone astray, Mehroo takes solace from the fact that Behram Roje was not over yet.

In an interview with Ali Lakhani, Rohinton Mistry comments,

> "Well, I suppose it does work in that way. In a sense this novel , will, when the Parsis have disappeared from the face of the earth, will preserve a record of how they fared, to some extent."

The comment was made in reference to his first novel *Such a Long Journey* which has a Parsi milieu. The novel is largely set in a Parsi housing estate, where –

> "The inhabitants of Khodadad Building are representatives of a cross- section of middle class Parsis expressing all the angularities of dwindling community. All the characters in the novel are individualized and memorably drawn with humour and compassion."[4]

The novel is centered on Gustad Noble, a Parsi Gentleman in his 50s. He lives along with his wife, Dilnawaz, their two sons Sohrab and Darius, and nine years old daughter, Roshan. Gusted has same close friends – Major Jimmy Bilimoria, Dinshawji and Tehmul Lungraa. Gustad works as a bank clerk and remains to his name 'Noble'. He is 'tall', 'solid', 'broad-shouldered', and 'very loyal' to his friends. He does not knowingly cause discomfort to anybody. He

> "is a pious Parsee whose life is governed by humata (good thoughts), hukhta (good words) and hvarshta (good deeds). His charitable act for the three destitute children his prayer for others at the church Mt. Mary are concrete illustrations of his probity and rectitude. Such little acts of kindness govern the best portion of his life."[5]

At times he gets nostalgic about his past when his father owned a bookstore and before him, his grandfather was the maker of fine furniture. Times were quite happy for them until fate intervened in the form of his uncle, who was entrusted with the responsibility of looking after the bookstore. But as luck would have it, he squandered the money, putting the family in dire circumstances – they were bankrupt. This resulted in the untimely death of his mother, who never recovered from the shock and lay in the hospital "uncomplaining and uncomprehending" ultimately letting go of her hold on life. He witnessed his father crying bitterly for having failed his family and resolved to never shed a tear himself.

Dilnavaz, affectionately called 'Dilnoo darling' by Gustad, is the typical Indian woman whose sole purpose in life is to look after her family's welfare. She leaves no stones unturned to that effect. She even takes the help of her neighbour, Miss Kutpitia, who claims to have indepth knowledge of spells, rituals and magic to possibly ward off the evil eye that surrounds her children. Once she even went to the extent of cutting Tehmul's dirty nails, collected them in a plastic dish and later burnt them over coals, like Gustad did for the loban thurible after his prayers were over in the evening. The obnoxious odour that emanated from the nails was "like the smell of the devil himself, from the depths of dojukh, she thought" (P.153) She believed in the good and civil aspects preached by Zoroastrianism and was simple enough to think that the evil eye can be cast away by snapping the fingers, pointing to the door, and saying *oowaryoo*. She also specialized in making traditional Parsi dishes like *dhansak* with *Kutchoomber* on Sundays, *dhandar – paatyo* and *pumpkin – buryani* an other occasions which were much appreciated by her family and others.

Sohrab is the eldest child of Gustad, the son on whom he had pinned all his hopes and aspirations – all that he could not achieve in life, he wanted to fulfill through the success of his son. Sohrab was the apple of his parents' eyes. But,

> "the seed of Sohrab's troubles had germinated long ago, long before last might, when his parents discovered how easily things came to their first- born, at home, in school at work or play. There seemed to be nothing Sohrab could not do, and do well. Whether it was arithmetic, or arts and crafts, or moral science, he bagged several prizes each year on Prize Distribution Day. ... before long, Gustad and Dilnavaz were convinced their son was very special. [SaLJ -64,65]

Thus grew the aspirations of Sohrab's parents for their son finally culminating in his getting through the entrance examination for IIT. But then Sohrab put his foot down finally on Roshan's ninth birthday, announcing to his thunderstruck father that he did not have any intentions of joining the IIT. Sohrab thinks of the past.

> "Daddy made pronouncements or dreamed dreams of an artist – son.It was never, my son will paint, my son will act, he will writepoetry. No, it was always – my son will be a doctor, he will bean engineer, he will be a research scientist. [SaLJ -66]

The situation is aptly summarized in Mistry's interview with Lakhani,

> Such a conflict between father and son – debating over the best choice of career for the latter was typical of the mindset of the 1960's and 1970s when science always got the preference over arts as far as studies for boys was concerned.[6]

Mistry here makes, what Meenakshi Mukherjee would say, a conscious use of the well known 'Sohrab – Rustom myth'.[7] Unlike the myth which ends on a tragic note, Mistry has a reconciliation of sorts between father and son in his own work. Gustad's carrying of Tehmul's not – so-light dead body single – handedly in spite of his limp, demonstrates to Sohrab not only his father's physical prowess but also an immense strength of spirit which ultimately effects the reconciliation. Narendra Kumar observes.

> "Thus while using a Zoroastrian myth in the narrative, Mistry Highlights the generation – gap which seems to threaten the very existence of Parsee family life."[8].

Gustad's second son, Darius, had a fascination for pets of all kinds and used to frequent Crawford market. To begin with, he got an assortment of fish – guppies, black mollies, kissing gouramis, and neontetra which died within a fortnight of being brought home. The next four years saw him getting

> "finches, sparrows, a squirrel, lovebirds, and a Nepali parrot, all of which succumbed to illnesses ranging from chest colds to mysterious growths in their craws that prevented eating and led to starvation". [SaLJ -43]

He used to cry bitterly after the death of each pet and ultimately got thoroughly disenchanted with the outside world.

> " .... A lack of good taste in whoever was responsible for such a pointless, wasteful finish: beautiful, colourful creatures, full of life and fun, hidden under the drab soii of the compound. What sense did it make ?" [SaLJ -43]

Through the experimentation and failure of Darius at keeping various pets, Mistry seeks to turn reader attention to the awareness in the Parsi community of the transitoriness of life, which logically brings on bodily suffering and decay. These important aspects of the Zoroastrian ethos are skillfully woven by Mistry in the narrative – perhaps the reason behind the creation of the character of Darius. He then turned his attention to body – building, which was his current preoccupation.

Very soon, however, he was down with a bout of pneumonia. This was interpreted by Miss Kutpitia as,

> "The innocent little fish and birds in his custody had no doubt cursed him with their dying breaths, and here, for all to see, was the result of their curses.' [SaLJ -43]

This statement points to the concepts of good *(Asha)* and evil *(Druj)* in Zoroastrianism, which are of paramount importance in the life of a Parsi. Darius had strayed on the wrong path, caused agony and suffering to innocent creatures, for which he was now made to suffer himself. Miss Kutpitia prescribed certain "remedies" to appease the dead animals.

Gustad's youngest child, his daughter, Roshan, has a very frail physical structure. She does not like to see her patents fighting, easily gets perturbed and eagerly tries to put an end to it. Gustad gets a live chicken to celebrate her ninth birthday. After the chicken has been fattened for two days, Roshan is visibly upset when the butcher slaughters it in their kitchen and does not eat it for her birthday dinner. Soon after, she falls seriously ill with some stomach infection and takes a pretty long time to heal. During her illness her father frequents Dr. Paymaster's Clinic and her mother abides by the advice of

Miss Kutpitia regarding 'other' forms of cure. Her long and protracted illness and Gustad's financial troubles in trying to provide for her prescribed expensive medicines are witness to the tests Gustad is subjected to. According to Geeta Doctor, the fastidious preoccupation with the body is peculiarly a Parsi trait. She is of the opinion that it reflects the preoccupation with illness that a community that knows that it is on the decline both fears and accepts.[9]

Major Jimmy Bilimoria, also a resident of Khodadad building, was a very close friend of Gustad. He was so close to the family of Gustad, that he was regarded as a brother more than a friend. A 'hot favourite' with the children, he was affectionately hailed as 'Major uncle' by them. They were urged 'to walk erect, with chest out and stomach in, like Major Uncle. (p. 13).

He often enthralls them with stories from his glorious army life – battles with Pakistan, etc. The fact that Gustad could not digest is the sudden, mysterious disappearance of the Major, without a word to anybody. He is missed terribly by Gustad, especially during the morning, when both of them used to pray together in the courtyard. But even after his disappearance from Khodadad building, he continues to influence Gustad's life in a major way. He sends word that he had again been called by the RAW to work for them on a secret mission and would send ten lakh rupees secretively which Gustad was to deposit in the bank under the name of 'Mira Obili'. As a special favour to a friend, Gustad agrees, however misgivingly, and with the help of Dinshawji, his friend and colleague in the bank begins the dangerous mission. The mission requires him to visit the infamous Chor-Bazaar of Bombay to meet the dangerous Gulam Mohammed who refers to Bilimoria as 'Bili Boy'. However, half-way through the deposits the events take another unexpected turn, when they learn of the Major's arrest in Delhi for embezzlement of Government funds. Gustad is instructed by the sinister looking Gulam Mohammed to return the entire money within 15 days, failing which Bilimoria's and consequently Gustad's life would be in danger. He does the needful and goes to meet the Major in a prison in Delhi where he is aghast both at Bilimoria's condition and the gruesome tale he narrates. He is further sentenced to four years' imprisonment, but dies of heart attack before the term is completed.

This incident is based on the real life incident of the infamous Sohrab Nagarwalla which rocked the Indira Gandhi Government.

> "In *Such a Long Journey* the Parsi world gradually moves out of its self- imposed isolation and interacts at the highest levels of finance and politics with the post colonial Indian world".[10]

Nagarwalla was the State Bank of India cashier who claimed that he had received a phone call from the then Prime Minister India Gandhi asking him to hand over a large sum of Rs. 60 lakhs to her messenger. However this story was not accepted to be true. Nagarwalla was subsequently arrested and died rather mysteriously before he could be brought to trial.

Viney Kirpal also suggests that Mistry subverts the 'official' version in *Such a long Journey.*[11] Mistry's novel vehemently challenges the authenticity of the official version of the report by offering an alternate one in the form of a footnote:

> "While the alleged facts of this case are certainly unique, what strikes this reporter as even more unusual are the circumstances surrounding this highly imaginative crime. For example, assuming that Mr. Bilimoria has the talent of voice impersonation, is it routine for our national banks to hand over vast sums of money if the Prime Minister telephones? How high does one have to be in the Government or the Congress party to be able to make such a call ? And was the Chief Cashier so familiar with Mrs. Gandhi's voice that he accepted the instruction without any verification whatsoever ? If yes does that mean Mrs. Gandhi has done this sort of thing frequently? These questions cry out for answers, and till the answers are heard, clearly and completely, the public's already eroded confidence in our leaders cannot be restored." [SaLJ 195-196]

Dinshawji is a close friend and colleague of Gustad. He has a nature which if not absolutely opposite, but quite different from that of Gustad's serious one. He is very outgoing, comic and quite irrepressible. He is described as a "jovial man" with a "quick tongue", one who is proud of his poetic abilities and regards himself as "Kavi Kamaal" and "Indian Tennyson". His penchant for the comic at times bordering on the obscene and indecent often made him unpopular among women. Critics have found his character objectionable. Interviewer Ali Lakhani mentions reviewer Constance Rooke as having said that his character Dinshawji may offend some feminist sensibilities. In his answer, Mistry said.

> "...... she is quite right. Dinshawji can offend me too. If I was to create characters mainly to satisfy, or to keep from offending, ... I would be creating cardboard cutouts."[12]

This interesting character, however, has been put to better use by Mistry – he is the mouthpiece for the insecurities felt by the Parsi minority community. A few examples from the novel are quoted below as examples:

> "What days those were, yaar. What fun we used to have ...... Parsis were the Kings of banking in those days. Such respect we used to get. Now the whole atmosphere only has been spoiled. Ever since that Indira nationalized the banks." [SaLJ -38]

> "Parsi crow-eaters, we'll show you who is the boss." [SaLJ -39]

> "Wait till the Marathas take over, then we will have real Gandoo Raj ...... All they know is to have rallies at Shivaji Park, shout slogans, make threats, and change road names. "[SaLJ -73]).

> "That was tragic ...... Even today, people say Feroze's heart attack was not really a heart a heart attack." [SaLJ -197]

Apart from these already discussed, there are other characters who are important to the narrative and worth mentioning. To begin with, there's Tehmul Lungraa, or Scrambled Egg as he is often called for his irritating habit of scratching particular parts of the body in a circular manner. He had a nasty fall from the solitary Neem tree in the compound as a child. That fall had been the undoing of his life – he was a child in a man's body. Mistry has deliberately contrasted his lameness and the subsequent conventional treatment, complete with working sticks and crutches to Gustad's accident – his fall from the bus to save his son, Sohrab, and the traditional, alternative treatment meted out by the Parsi Madhiwala Bonesetter. Apart from the slight limp, Gustad could lead a normal life, while Tehmul was maimed forever. Says Nilufer Bharucha,"Here we have Mistry lauding the older ways of living and healing from his distant diasporic location. Is this an act of nostalgia?"[13]

Miss Kutpitia, "the ubiquitous witch" is a woman in her seventies. She is a spinster, by choice and has remained in mourning ever since the death of her brother and his child in an accident. She had taken it upon herself to look after the boy's needs since the death of his mother. But when he too was snatched away by the cruel hands of fate, she could not bear the shock. People talked about her as being rich, but eccentric – the spinster who lived alone, but had dark secrets in the form of the two dead bodies inside her flat. She does not cry any more, her tears having dried up long ago. N.P. Sharma aptly describes her condition.

> "The centuries of suffering, segregation and loneliness have brought the to a vision of life where nothing is amiss and perhaps this is how they are ready even for their extinction."[14]

Dinshawji also caters to this description of Parsis who suffer willingly, uncomplainingly and for a long time. He only makes a passing reference to his domestic woes by calling his wife, Alamai, as 'my domestic vulture' or

> "Better that my dear domestic vulture eats me up than the feathered ones.

With her I have a guarantee – she at least won't scatter pieces of my meat all over Bombay." [SaLJ -72]

Another eccentric Parsi is old Cavasji, in his late eighties who was in the habit of coming out in the balcony, looking up at the sky, and hurling "cosmic criticisms" reprimanding God for being unjust and unfair.

"To the Tatas you give so much! And nothing for me ? To the Wadias you give, you keep on giving! You cannot hear my prayers? The pockets of the Camas only you will fill ! We others don't need it, you think?" [SaLJ -87]

Other minor characters include Inspector Bamji, who was "fond of verbal colour and ribaldry" and always saying "*umcha section nai";* Mr. Rabadi, who was nicknamed" the Dogwalla idiot" by Gustad because of his habit of bringing his dog on a leash to the vinca and *Subjo* bushes of Gustad at night; Dr. Paymaster, whom Gustad went to from his childhood days and who could not practice under his actual name but in the name of one Dr. Lord, from whom he had bought the clinic and Dr. Paymaster has been described as a "sad clown doctoring in his jesterly way"; and last but not the least, Peerbhoy Paan – walla, who sold his 'paan' near the 'house-of-cages' – the red light area and claimed to have a 'paan' for all occasions, the most in demand being the 'palung-tode-paan'.

In this first novel of Mistry's there are only three non-Parsi characters – Malcolm Saldanha, the Christian, a very dear child hood friend of Gustad with whom he even goes to the Church of Mount Mary to pray; Gulam Mohammed the Muslim the taxi driver who had brought him home safely from the site of accident, who later turned out to be working with RAW like Major Bilimoria; and the pavement artist who eventually graduates to a wall artist on Gustad's advice – expectedly his religion is not mentioned. He is commissioned by Gustad to paint pictures of various gods and goddesses – pertaining to all faiths, on the compound wall encircling Khodadad building. The wall in question, was a source of constant nuisance to the inmates of Khodadad building;

"The flies, the mosquitoes, the horrible stink, with bloody shameless people pissing, squatting alongside the wall. Late at night it became like a wholesale public latrine." [SaLJ -16]

Many pages later, we have Mistry's voice through the pavement artist's underlining another tenet of Zoroastrianism – the Zoroastrian World view which implies that,

"A true Parsee should be tolerant about the faiths and beliefs of others. Zoroastrianism makes them sociable with the other sister communities of India."[15]

The pavement artist (Mistry?) says:

"There is no difficulty... using assorted religious and their gods, saints and prophets : Hindu, Sikh, Judaic, Christian, Muslim, Zoroastrian, Buddhist, Jainist. Actually, Hinduism alone can provide enough. But I always like to mix them up, include a variety in my drawings. Makes me feel I am doing something to promote tolerance and understanding in the world".[SaLJ -182]

The wall of all religious came into existence due to the persistent efforts of the artist, a BA in world Religions. The inhabitants of Khodadad building are expectedly happy to at last breathe fresh air. Gulam Mohammed too does his bit to promote religious tolerance – he arranges for the last rites of Major Bilimoria to be held at The Tower of silence, though not allowed to be party to the procedure. Avadhesh Kumar Singh observes,

"..... The novel [*Such a Long Journey*] as a cluster of narratives, centralizes his [Mistry's] community as a protagonist. There is constant dialogical interaction between stories about the past and the present of the Parsi community,and Mistry like his counterparts [Firdaus Kanga, Farukh Dhondy and Bapsi Sidhwa] informs the past of his community, comments on its present and anticipates the flow of events to follow through its characters."[16]

Against the gamut of Parsi Character with their oddities and eccentricities in *Such a Long Journey*, Mistry's Commonwealth writers Prize winning second novel, *A Fine*

Balance, can boast of relatively fewer characters of the said Parsi minority community. The novel revolves around two Parsi characters, Dina Dalal, a widow, and Maneck Kohlah, her paying guest, and two *chamars* – turned – tailors who work for Dina. Apart from them there are the families of Dina and Maneck in the background who form the wide canvas of the novel, set against the backdrop of the Internal Emergency imposed by the then Prime Minister, Indira Gandhi in 1975. An attempt has been made here to examine the Parsiness of the Parsi characters. It will be appropriate to quote here, at the outset, contradictory opinions of critics regarding this fact. Sudha P.Pandya, in her comparative study of Meena Alexander's *Nampally Road* and Rohinton Mistry's *A Fine Balance* is of the opinion that: "However, the exclusive Parsi ethos of the earlier works is missing."[17]

Savita Goel, in her critique of *A Fine Balance,* however feels:

> "In this novel, like his earlier works, the writer once again succeeds in recreating Parsi ambience. The rich culture, customs and traditions of the marginalized Parsi community are foregrounded and scenes describing the Parsi death rites and funeral ceremonies give the reader a glimpse into the Parsi world view."[18]

Jaydipsinh Dodiya's article, "Rohinton Mistry's *A Fine Balance: A Diasporic Novel*" published in *Parsi Fiction*, Vol. 2, ed. Novy Kapadia p. 212, 2001 voices the same sentiments in (surprisingly) exactly the same words (???) as Savita Goel's article mentioned above in 1998.

This particular point, portrayed in different ways by critics needs closer examination - is *A Fine Balance* a 'Parsi' book like Mistry's preceding works of fiction or isn't it ?

In *A Fine Balance,* the reader is pleasantly surprised to find a woman, Dina Dalal, nee Shroff, at the helm of affairs, unlike Mistry's earlier works. She is introduced in the Prologue as a widow of Rustam Dalal. Two tailors, Ishvar and Omprakash Darji and a young student, Maneck Kohlah reach her small, shabby flat together. The tailors have come in search of work and Maneck for paying guest accommodation. The four main characters of the narrative are thus introduced in the 'Prologue: 1975', which ends on a note of optimism.

The first chapter has Dina reminiscing about her past – childhood, youth and the life that has gone by. Her father was a doctor and in his lifetime Dina has a very sheltered and pampered childhood. Her woes begin with his sudden and untimely death which leaves the twelve year old Dina hapless and without a pillar to lean on, especially with her mother becoming more and more reclusive and increasingly uncomprehending of things around her. Dina helps her in her daily chores and even takes leave from school to accompany her mother to the Fire Temple to offer prayers for her father. However, the lewd behaviour of the priest, Dustoor Framji towards Dina (and all young girls) leaves a bitter taste in her month – so much so that she does not go to the fire temple of her own accord in her childhood or even on growing up. She is so completely disillusioned with his behaviour that for her marriage ceremony with Rustom, she prefers to stay clear of him. Dustoor Framji, who has earned the reputation of being called Dustoor Daab-Chaab, voices his grievances thus:

> "For death they come to me – for seros-mu-partare, for afargan, baaj, faroksry. But for a happy occasion, for wedding ashirvad, I am not wanted." [AFB-45]

This is one of the few occasions in the narrative when Mistry indulges in high-lighting Parsi customs. Unfortunately for Dina, Rustom dies on their third marriage anniversary. Her world comes crashing down, but she conducts herself in a very dignified manner, stays with her brother's family for some time, and later shifts to Rustom's flat, to live independently, by herself. Rustom's relatives, Shirin Aunty and Darab Uncle help her in getting some tailoring assignments. During these jobs, she comes in contact with some idiosyncratic members of the Parsi community. The Munshis were the best because they paid promptly. The Parekhs liked to haggle, Mr. Savukshaw spent a lot of his money on the bottle, so it was advisable to collect advance payment from them. The Surtees were a very ridiculous pair – Mrs. Surtee was in the habit of burning up all of Mr. Surtee's pyjamas whenever they had an argument and served him the ashes collected on a plate for dinner. This process resulted in ordering many pairs of pyjamas at a time but, Dina was advised to pretend noting was amiss. Other names taken are Davars, Kotwals, Mehtas, Pavris, Vatchas and Seervais. But they are only introduced in name on page 67 of the novel, with no direct meeting with Dina being put on record. An important bit of advice imparted to Dina by Shirin Aunty was not to measure the men for their inseams in isolation lest they take advantage of the situation. Dina's business meetings with a Parsi bachelor, Freedoon, is described ever the next few pages. These meetings, however, verge on friendship, which soon develops into a more intimate relationship – Dina and Freedoon become lovers. Here, however, Mistry takes the opportunity to highlight a Zoroastrian belief of the sanctity of marriage.

> "According to Zoroastrianism, a true marriage is the sacred union of two souls, competing with each other in the ideal practice of self-abnegation. The marriage – ritual is also symbolic; fire which is present at the agreement – stage, is taken as the witness to the union of the two souls."[19]

In keeping with this principle of marriage in mind, Dina has certain reservations even though she takes Fredoon as a lover:

> "But when they ventured into the private garden of intimacy, it was a troubled relationship. There were certain things she could not bring herself to do. The bed-any bed-was out of bounds, sacred and reserved for married couples only". [AFB-73]

Another Parsi belief highlighted by Mistry through the trials of Dina as a widow is the bad omen of getting hair cut within the premises of one's dwelling place. Dina was in touch with her school friend, Zenobia who had become successful as a hair stylist. Zenobia taught Dina the basics of hair-cutting and advised her to visit the homes of relatives and friends to provide an easier hair-cut for their children within the comfort of their homes. This endeavour, however, proved futile, for people retaliated with:

> "Madam, you have no consideration ? What have we done to you that you want to bring misfortune within our four walls ?" [AFB-72]

And again,

> "Some people did offer her their children's heads. 'But only if you do it outside; they said. Dina refused. There were limits to what she would do. She was a in home children's stylist, not an open – air pavement barber." [AFB-72]

These incidents bring to mind an incident from Dina's Childhood, when she had defied Nusswan and with the help of Zenobia had cut off her long plaits in school, in favour of a shorter hair style which was in fashion. Nusswan had retaliated in quite a similar manner:

> "I don't want another word from you ...... Take a bath first, you polluted creature ! Wash off those hair clippings before you spread them around the house and bring misfortune upon us!" [AFB-28]

When Dr. Shroff died, Nusswan was almost twice the age of his sister, Dina. He assumed the role of head of the family, sold off his father's dispensary, and started controlling the family's finances. He decided to relieve the live-in-servant, Lily, and by his wily ways made Dina do all the housework. This resulted in her poor performance at school. He decided to stop her studies. This resulted in a bitter fight between them. Acts like these on Nusswan's part were against the Zoroastrian tenets, which preach:

> "The true Zoroastrian way of life consists in spreading happiness around. ... A true Parsee lives not for himself but for his family, society and the country as a whole. ... Men and women are given equal status in every sphere of life. Both have equal opportunities of spiritual evolution and salvation."[20]

Nusswan's despotic behaviour, his strict discipline bordering on the tyrannical, beating up his little sister, making her work like a domestic drudge, in short making her life miserable is against the basic tenets of his religion. The situation seems all the more ironic, when he takes her (Dina) to the fire-temple to pray – for her welfare. Dina finds the whole exercise ludicrous:

> " While she bowed before the sanctum, he travelled along the outer wall hung with pictures of various dustoors and high priests. He glidedfrom display to display, stroking the garlands, hugging the frames, kissing the glass, and ending with the very tall picture of Zarathustra to which he glued his lips for a full minute. Then, from the vessel of ashes placed in the sanctum's doorway, he smeared a pinch on his forehead, another bit across the throat, and undid his top two shirt buttons to rub a fistful over his chest. Like talcum powder, thought Dina." [AFB-24]

Mistry seems to be laughing at Nusswan for his religious absurdities, as if to say, smearing the holy ashes over the body will only make him believe that he is being purified – but would it, really?

It is not that Nusswan is totally painted in black by Mistry. He also has a humane side to his personality. He went out of his way (unexpectedly for Dina) to arrange a good party for Dina's marriage. When she become a widow after a short married life of three years, he very sympathetically and affectionately brought her back home and took good care of her. But his good behaviour was a very transient phase. It disappeared soon after she started rejecting proposals for her marriage suggested by him. Nilufer Bharucha describes this as:

> "Very soon, her numbness and Nusswan's sympathy wear off and the brother and sister indulge in a typical *Parsi* exchange of invectives and insults."[21]

My objection is to the word Parsi used here by Bharucha. Is it not a very natural and universal phenomenon for a brother and sister pair to fight in this manner? In my opinion through the bitter verbal exchange quoted below, Mistry is highlighting the feeling of superiority of Parsis over other Indian communities which is mentioned later by Bharucha. Nusswan says,

> "Do you know how fortunate you are in our community ? Among the unenlightened, widow's are thrown away like garbage. If you were a Hindu, in the old days you would have to be a good little sati and leap onto your husband's funeral pyre, be roasted with him." [AFB-63,64]

Nusswan's wife, Ruby, does not have any claims to the good looks that Dina is blessed with. She is rather dark complexioned, which is quite unusual among Parsis who pride themselves on their frail complexion and good looks. There is an incident when. Nusswan is summoned by his old grandfather to visit him. He does so, along with wife Ruby, and sister, Dina, who had in the first place lodged a complaint against him. Ruby had been instructed by Nusswan to please the old man. So when Ruby started massaging the feet of Nusswan's old Grandfather, he reacted unpredictably –

> "Enraged, he tore his foot from her grasp. ' Kya Karta hai? Chalo, Jao!' Too startled at being addressed in Hindi, Ruby sat there gaping. Grandfather turned to Nusswan, 'Doesn't she understand? What language does your ayah speak? Tell her to get off my sofa, wait in the kitchen.' Ruby rose in a huff and stood by the door. 'Rude old man!' she hissed. 'Just because my skin is little dark!, "[AFB-28]

This is an example of Parsi feeling of superiority so deeply imbued in the older generation, which is very difficult to shake off. Ruby's reaction too is interesting. She is shocked to be spoken to in Hindi. For the Parsis, it is either 'their' language Gujarati (which they had accepted long ago) or English – with which they had increasingly started identifying themselves with. Hindi is to be spoken to people who did not understand Parsi – Gujarati or English – the lesser Indians (for eg. the uneducated ayah who Ruby was mistaken to be).

When Dina's schooling was abruptly truncated by Nusswan, she hungers for knowledge. This hunger takes her to the public libraries! Some of which were equipped with music rooms. Slowly, but surely, she starts educating herself. Music provided the much needed solace her soul was looking for. She started attending free concerts. It was at these concerts that she met her future husband, Rustom. It is interesting to note here that Mistry, in an interviews with Angela Lambaert, has said that he had met his wife Freny at a music school.

> 'where she was taking voice and piano lessons and I was doing classes in music theory and composition'[22]

During their courting before marriage, Rustom remarks :

> "Like all good Parsi parents, mine made me take violin lessons, when I was little, he laughed." [AFB-40]

About some 68 pages out of a total of some 752 have been devoted to the first chapter entitled city by the sea where Dina's life with its Parsi background has been described by Mistry. The next three chapters detail the tailors' lives, their history with all its caste ridden oppressions in the village, their training and turning into darjis from chamars, their eventual arrival in the city to try out their luck, their working for Dina Dalal and the various trials and tribulations regarding food and lodging in the expensive city. The Parsi thread is again picked up by Mistry three chapters and some 152 pages later. The fifthchapter, entitled Mountains is set in an un-named hill station where the family of Maneck Kohlah stay. The mountainous regions with its snow-covered peaks and misty mornings are described most lovingly and in details.

Farokh and Aban Kohlah, parents of Maneck, own a small shop, which is part of their house. It is a kind of departmental store with a good business, especially with its brand of Kohlah's cola, which has a secret formula handed down from one generation to another. The Kohlah family loves the pure mountain air and water and everything associated with it, even though there are limited opportunities available there. Maneck has a major disagreement with his father regarding his studies.

As a child he is sent to a boarding school, which he bitterly resents. After finishing school, his father suggests he goes to study refrigeration and Air-conditioning in the city for a secure future. Maneck reads it as if his father wants to send him away – make him do something he does not like. This misunderstanding between father and son is similar to the one in Mistry's first novel where Sohrab has a tough time convincing his father, Gustad, that he is not interested in joining the IIT. In that story Sohrab shows adamancy and walks out in anger, whereas Maneck allows himself to be over-ruled by his father and holds a grudge against him. This troubled relationship between father and son is in keeping with the generation – gap which is shaking the foundation of Parsi family life. In a similar vein, Nusswan too declares his unwillingness in becoming a doctor like his father, preferring to go into business and eventually sells off his father's dispensary on his death. The father-son conflict is symbolic of the Parsi life in a state of transition.

Farokh Kohlah is a victim of the partition of India, which created a separate Pakistan.

> "A foreigner drew a magic line on a map and called it the new border; it became a river of blood upon the earth. And the orchards, fields, factories, businesses, all on the wrong side of that line, vanished with a wave of the pale conjuror's wand." [AFB-248,249]

The tremendous diminishing of family fortunes was borne with a brave exterior by him. However, fate was cruel to him once again, this time in the guise of modernization of roads and further development of the nation.

> "Mr. Kohlah watched helplessly as the asphalting began, changing the brown rivers into black, completing the transmogrification of his beloved birthplace where his forefathers had lived as in paradise. He watched powerlessly while, for the second time, lines on paper ruined the life of the Kohlah family, only this time it was an indigenous surveyer's cartogram not a foreigner's imperial map." [AFB-263]

Charu C. Mishra describes Farokh's condition:

"More than anybody else Farokh Kohlah is shocked to the core of his heart. He feels as if he has been displaced from his dear land once again. The devastation of nature around him makes him depressed and terrified."[23]

This 'displacement' from the 'dear land' could also be extended to the displacement of the Parsis from their mother land – Iran – a fact which every Parsis still feels nostalgic about, thought it was their forefathers who actually went through the turmoil. Mistry seems to be pointing in a veiled manner to this depression, insecurity and fear which has become part of the Parsi psyche.

Farokh Kohlah though being a quiet, peace – loving man in his later years, can also be described as a person who is very strong willed and at times even defies the dictates of religion. His final wish of a funeral in the Hindu way, would enable his family to scatter his ashes all over the mountainside, so that he would totally merge with the environment he loved so much. Charu C. Mishra observes:

"Primarily, his wish for cremation was an outraging one as his religion Zoroastrianism prescribes the disposal of dead body by feeding it to vultures. Anticipating that any left out part of his body might further defile the land, he even dares to violate the sanction of his religion."[24].

Mistry seizes the opportunity to comment on a very important custom of Zoroastrianism – their last act of charity, of offering their dead body to the hungry vultures – nature's scavengers. With many Parsis having spread out to all parts of the world from their base in Gujarat and Bombay, it is becoming increasingly difficult to follow the primitive system of cremation. So as to preserve its sanctity, Mrs. Kohlah explains to her son, Maneck, how it had been difficult to find dastoors for the prayers at the time of cremation:

"How narrow – minded these people are, 'she said, shaking her head. 'of course we are cremating because it was

Daddy's wish, but what about people who cannot afford to transport the body? Would these peiests deny them the prayers ?" [AFB-715]

During the British rule the Parsis identified themselves so much with the colonisers, that at times they were in 'danger of over-identification with the British'. Everything English was considered to be not only good but the best among available options. This point finds reflection in the following extract from the text:

> "When these retired brigadiers, majors, and colonels came to tea at the Kohlahs', they arrived suited and booted, as they called it, with watches in their fabs and ties around their necks. These trappings might have seemed comical to a nationalist bent of mind but had talismanic value for their wearers. It was all that stood between them and the disorder knocking at the door. Mr. Kohlah himself was partial to bow ties. Mrs. Kohlah served the tea an Aynsley bone china; the cutlery was Sheffield. If it was a special dinner at Navroze or Khardad Sal, she used the Wedge wood set." [AFB-254]

Bharucha observes,

> "...... by the end of the nineteenth century, well-to-do Parsi families had became greatly anglicized. Their homes had become cluttered with heavy curved rosewood and teak furniture and Victorian bric a brac."[25]

Bharucha's observation and the corresponding extract from the text substantiates the importance Parsis attach to articles of British origin that even celebration of special Parsi days are complete with the corresponding and special 'English' touch.

Maneck Kohlah can never reconcile himself to the fact that his parents, specially his father, have sent him far away from the hills he loved so much, to study a 'technical' course that they valued so much, but he did not think much of. The result is his unhappiness at being removed from familiar, lovable surroundings, in the same manner in which his father, Farokh, is perpetually unhappy with first the partition and then the much loved hills being brutally scarred in the name of modernization. The behaviour of father and son are reflective of nostalgia and uneasiness of Parsi psyche at large – of having been displaced from the land of their ancestors.

The character of Maneck embodies another important aspect of Zoroastrianism – a feeling of brotherhood for all human beings. Narendra Kumar asserts:

> "The true Zoroastrian way of life consists in spreading happiness around. A Parsee should regard himself as part and parcel of nature, and as such, fulfill his obligation towards all creation. A true Parsee lives not for himself but for his family, society, and the country as a whole. Brotherhood of man is thus a cardinal doctrine of Zoroaster's message."[26]

In keeping with this sentiment his sympathy for the tailors is understandable. He empathises with their situation from day one of their meeting when he shares his glass of watermelon – sherbet with them, gauging very quickly that they very well cannot afford one. Later, when circumstances force the tailors to seek shelter in Dinabai's flat, she agrees to provide them with food as well, which they will eat on the verandah. To this Maneck replies,

> "Fine. In that case, I'll also eat on the verandah. I cannot take part in such an insult. My father feeds only stray dogs on the porch." [AFB-485]

This stand of Maneck is praiseworthy and Dina Dalal also can be excused for this misdemeanor on her part taking into consideration her behaviour with the tailors as the narrative progresses. She does not make distinctions among cups for herself and the tailors as she did in the past. In the chapter entitled 'Sailing Under One Flag', they really do so, moving aside all distinctions of caste, creed, religion and social hierarchy. On yet another occasion, Maneck asserts that the leftovers from dinner should be fed to the stray cats who are hungry outside, rather than thrown in the garbage pail -thus extending his charity to the mute animals, treating them in the same humane manner that his father used with stray dogs.

Another example of the Zoroastrian world view manifest in the character of Maneck is seen in the manner in which he decides to join in the funeral procession of Shankar, a beggar by professlon, who was better known as 'the worm'. When Dina could not persuade him to stay out of it, she too went along with him – to be a part of the cremation procedure of a beggar, who was also a wonderful human being. Narendra Kumar observation is noteworthy:

> "They mix freely with members of other faiths, sympathise with them in their griefs and afflictions and work to alleviate their miser."[27]

Apart from these, there are only a few other minor incidents where Mistry stresses on the Parsiness of characters – there are hardly other Parsi characters than the ones already mentioned worth discussing. Apart from the 68 pages in the first chapter and some others in the fifth which centers around the Parsiness of Maneck's family, there are relatively few pages devoted by Mistry to discussions exclusively on the Parsi family. In the beginning of the discussion, two contradictory opinions of critics on the some topic had been mentioned. A thorough reading of the novel upholds Sudha Pandya's opinion over Savita Goel and Jaydipsinh Dodiya's – 'the exclusive Parsi ethos of Mistry's earlier works is missing'. To put it into other words,

> "*A Fine Balance* represents on expansion from the previous tight focus on Parsi communities in Mistry's work and gives space for other social perspectives. What Nila Shah describes as 'a proliferation of" alternative histories of the excluded "produces a pluralist anarchy on the one hand and recreates the nation it belongs to on the other?"[28]

In Mistry's third novel, *Family Matters,* published, in 2002, the focus is again on the Parsi world in Bombay. Set in the mid - 1990s, a middle- class Parsi family with its trials and tribulations is the area of Mistry's Interest. Speaking about the origins of *Fancily Matters,* Mistry acknowledges to interviewer John Bemrose,

> "As far as I can tell, the novel started with the old man," the author says, referring to the ailing Nariman, the central character in *Family Matters,* whose care puts such a burden on his Bombay family. "The very first story I wrote for *Tales From Firozsha Baag* was told in an old man's, voice. I think I must have enjoyed doing that, and wanted to do it again."[29]

Sooni Taraporewala, a freelance photojournalist and scriptwriter, whose photograph was chosen for the front cover of Mistry's *Family Matters* says:

> "This picture was taken in April 1984 on Avan roj of Avan mahino, which is the one day in the year when Parsis pray beside any water body. I don't know the gentleman in the sola topee ... This picture appears on the cover of all the international editions of author Rohinton Mistry's back *Family Matters.*"[30]

Nariman Vakeel, the 79 year old Patriarch, a widower, with Parkinson's disease, holds centre stage. He stays with his step children, Coomy and Jal in his flat housed in Chateau Felicity, a Parsi baag. Coomy and Jal are middle aged and step children of Nariman, who had married their mother, Yasmin, after their father's death. This kind of a family set up might seem to be unusual to western readers, but quite a commonality in India, where unmarried adult children continue to live with their parents. Those children who remain unmarried also have to shoulder the responsibility of their aged, ailing and uncooperative (due to old age parents). Their half-sister, Roxana who married and set up her own home with her husband Yezad, is therefore, resented by Coomy for not having to care for their father. Nilufer Bharucha draws attention to the fact that:

> ".... A rampant individualism that does not brook the adjustments required within marriage, have led to most Parsis not marrying at all..."[31]

This phenomenon along with the fact that prices of property in the places generally inhabited by the Parsi Community are quite high lead to the uncomfortable situation in which Coomy and Jal found themselves in. Coomy tries to lay down rules for Nariman's conduct around the house –

> "... prohibition against locked doors, he was required to announce his intention to use the W.C. In the morning he was not to get out of bed till she came to get him ...... There were more rules regarding his meals his clothes, his dentures, his use of the radiogram....." [FM 2}

The brother –sister duo also vehemently protest Nariman's evening walks citing examples of newspaper reports of atrocities towards aged Parsis. This is however objected to by Bharucha saying that it "is a danger experienced by other senor citizens in Bombay, not just the elderly Parsis"[32]. And continuing in this vein, She has a dig at Mistry for relying heavily on newspaper reports, as he does to get information on the years he has been away – as acknowledged in an interview.

Nariman's seventy-ninth birthday is celebrated with Roxana arriving with her husband Yezad and two sons, Murad and Jehangir. During the evening, however, Nariman manages to annoy Coomy, who starts cribbing about the past, blames Nariman for all the unhappiness and mentions Lucy Braganza. Jahangir and Murad question their parents on their way back and readers are informed of resistance within the Parsi community to inter-religious marriages.

> ".... Grandpa had wanted to marry Lucy, but couldn't because she was not a Parsi. So he married uncle and Aunty's mother ... He asked if there was a law against marrying someone who wasn't a Parsi. His father said yes, the law of bigotry..." [FM 42]

Bharucha, herself a Parsi, however argues that this is not a phenomenon peculiar to Parsis and cites parallels in the world, in the USA, Black/White marriages and Britain, White/ Asian marriages which are still not welcome. She opines;

> "This is not a Defence of Parsi orthodoxy but merely an attempt to set the record straight that Parsis are not unique in being allergic to their offspring marrying outside their community."[33]

While on the topic of Parsi marriages, it would be appropriate to mention here another debatable matter relevant to this fact, which has still not found headway in the Parsi community. This refers to the ongoing controversy regarding acceptance/non-acceptance of children born of Parsi women marrying outside the Parsi community. These children are not accepted into the Parsi fold. This principle, however, does not apply to the children of Parsi men marrying non-Parsi women. Nariman's father had once taken objection to a Zoroastrian priest's performing the *Navjote* for children of Parsi women and non- Parsi men. These objections, voiced through letters in newspaper columns, met with objections from his neighbour, Mr. Arjani, also an inhabitant of Chateau Felicity. Nariman's father in one such letter, referred to Mr. Arjani as:

> "... A prime example of the substandard mind whose cogitations were clearly worthless, unable to grasp the simplest tenets of the religion and the supreme significance of the Navjote." [FM 133]

Narendra Kumar observes in *Parsee Novel*:

> "Thought Prophet Zoroaster rejected ritualism, certain rituals are central to Parsee life, since they are invested with symbolic significance. Among the rituals in Parsee life, *Navjote* ceremony is the most significant one. Between seven and fifteen years of age, a Parsee boy or girl has to pass through this rite of initiation, formally embracing the religion of Zarathustra."[34]

The *Navjote* ceremony, therefore is of the same significance as *Baptism* in Christianity. In the case of Coomy and Jal, the *Navjot* had been performed earlier than usual, as a special consideration for Palonji, their father, affected by Tuberculosis, who did not have much longer to live. In *Such a Long Journey*, Mistry's first novel, Sohrab's Navjot is also mentioned as an occasion to cherish and remember.

After the Navjot ceremony, the initiate is presented with the *Sudreh,* a spotless white shirt, and *Kusti*, made of lamb's wool, tied around the waist, dividing the upper and lower parts of the body. These are the two emblems of the Zoroastrian faith. Mistry's *Such a Long Journey,* befittingly begins with mentions of Ahura Mazda, and *Kusti* prayers and again on pages 4 and 5 the *Kusti* is described in detail, how Gustad felt a great peace of mind and empowered against the evils of the world. At the side of Tehmul's dead body, Gustad repeatedly recites the Yatha Ahu Varyo and Ashene Vahoo as much for the peace of the departed soul, and all those for whom he had not shed tears, and as much for himself. In Mistry's third novel Yezad is shown to be a non-believer of rituals and feels,

> "going to the fire-temple on Navroze and Khardad Sal was enough for him, and loban smoke was merely one way to get rid of mosquitoes. "[FM 25]

When Nariman is brought to Yezad's house with a broken ankle, without any previous intimation by Coomy and Jal, he finds it rather difficult to provide for the extra expenses. He is gradually found making his way to the fire temple in search of solace. Roxana is happy at first to see this change in Yezad but his inclination towards religion soon borders on the extreme, making life uneasy for those around. The bookshelves in the bedroom are filled with 'Volumes of Parsi History and Zoroastrianism, "Various translations of the Zend-Avesta, ... "[FM 463]

The change in Yezad is slow, but sure and complete. He has turned very orthodox in his religious practices. He does not work anymore. The investments from the proceedings of the sale of the flat keep the household going. Yezad has cordoned off an area in the dressing room solely for his religious practices. Roxana is not allowed entry into that area or kitchen during her menstrual cycle. He has joined 'The League of Orthodox Parsis and the Association for Zarathustrian Education" [FM 466]. He keeps having arguments with his elder son Murad who calls him a bigot, like Hitler, in reaction to Yezad's assertion "Because we are a pure Persian race, a unique contribution to this planet, and mixed marriages will destroy that". [FM 483] Ironically enough Murad has been found to be dating a non-Parsi girl, which Yezad has taken a strong objection to.

The Epilogue details many customs of the Parsi community, Murad's eighteenth birthday celebrated twice – one on the Parsi roj, according to the Zoroastrian calender, and the other according to the English calender. All details, right down to the floor decorated with a fish motif in white chalk, Murad being presented with the symbols of good luck and prosperity : betel leaves and betel – nuts, dates, flowers, a coconut' [FM 497], vermilion teelo applied on the forehead, etc. are meticulously provided by Mistry. Roxana sees to it that Murad's eighteenth birthday is celebrated in traditional Parsi style along with Parsi sweets – Sooterfeni, burfi, malai-na-khaja, from the Parsi dairy farm.

Yezad's character has undergone a complete transformation under Mistry's pen - from a very rational, down-to-earth character he becomes a religious fanatic. At one time he had nurtured hopes and made concrete efforts to migrate to Canada. All his efforts, however, were in vain as Yezad had been rudely turned down by the immigration authorities. He had put the entire correspondence safely away and his family took pride in the very eloquent manner the letters had been composed. Yezad's endeavours to migrate to Canada are reminiscent of Mistry's own (though successful) ones. In accordance with the first two novels, the third novel also has the writer's comments on 'useful' education. Yezad tells his son, Jehangir :

> "Study useful things – computers, M.B.A., and they'll welcome you. Not useless things like me, history and literature and philosophy." [FM 45]

It will be appropriate to note here, that Mistry's second degree in graduation – a B.A. in English Literature and Philosophy from the University of Toronto, with its exposure to literary heavyweights helped him evolve into the writer that he is. It is possible that Mistry seems to be making a point here through subtle irony.

Mistry, in his third novel, *Family Matters,* uses the central character of Nariman to put on record several customs and beliefs particular and peculiar to the Parsi community. Nariman keeps the children entertained with stories from the Shah-Nama and his own childhood. He talks about his childhood friend, Nauzer, whose family had a great love for animals and how they had many dogs and birds as pets. Mistry takes this opportunity to mention that Parsis have a great aversion for cats as they hate water and never take a bath; Parsis don't kill spiders and they only eat the female chicken, never a cock. At Jehangir's behest, Nariman relates the whole story of the evil king Zuhaak, who had two massive serpents growing from his shoulders, which had to be satiated with the brains of two young men everyday. After about nine hundred years of misery, deliverance came in the form of Faridoon, who fought with great courage, ultimately managing to bury Zuhaak inside Mount Damavand, Zuhaak strives throughout the night to break apart his chains, which the cock announces every morning. In answer, the spider is promptly sent to strengthen the chains by spinning its web.

Speaking of Parsi baags in an interview, Mistry had answered that he had the chance to observe them closely by virtue of having some friends who lived in them. In his first novel there is Khodadad building, a Parsi housing enclave, with its various idiosyncratic Parsi characters. His second novel, however, is bereft of any such 'baag'. It seems he makes up for this void by providing not one, but two such interesting locations. The first is Chateau Felicity where first Nariman's parents and then he along with wife Yasmin and their children Coomy, Jal and Roxana lived. It is also the building where the unfortunate incident involving his wife, Yasmin, and beloved, Lucy takes place- they fall together to their deaths. It is also the building which Nariman bequeaths to Coomy and Jal and from where he is strategically turned out by his step children. Coomy and Jal unceremoniously dump Nariman in Roxana's tiny flat, which is housed in another Parsi baag – Pleasant Villa. As against the seven – roomed magnificent flat of Chateau Felicity, the one in Pleasant Villa consists of two small rooms, a tiny balcony a kitchen, and a toilet. The circumstances though being crammed, the family is never the less happy. People are meant to be happy in Pleasant Villa – Mistry's penchant for labeling, rather than naming. When the Chenoy family take a conscious decision to move in with Jal on Coomy's death, which they are forbidden to do by Nariman, life becomes everything but happy for the small but once happy family of four. As is natural in such close surroundings, nothing remains hidden from the neighbours, and Yezad comments:

> "... This now was real window- shopping : by keeping an eye on the basket- on- a - rope commerce, you could tell who was eating what on any given day." [FM 115, 116]

This was said by way of explaining, how it was the practice of one Mr. Engineer, who lived on second floor, to skillfully take away an egg everyday from the basket going past his window, meant for the neighbour who lived above. Mistry's answer to interviewer Ali Lakhani on this aspect of the Parsi baag is quite pertinent:

> "Western eyes after all see this close knit community and the neighbourliness as something very positive, something laudable. And at the same time it can be claustrophobic and intrusive – one has no sense of privacy. Everybody knows everyone else's business."[35]

This claustrophobia is inherent in Gustad's reaction, in *Such a Long Journey* when he is upset with Sohrab.He even resorts to hitting him with the belt:

> "Enough is enough! This is sleeping-time, not fighting - time! Save the rest for morning !"The voice was Miss. Kutpitia's...Gustad was furious. He rushed to the window. "Come to my door and speak if you have something to say! I am not living free here, I also pay rent !" [SaLJ -51]

The flat in Pleasant Villa was a wedding gift to Roxana from her father. As already noted she leads a comparatively happy, though constrained life in Pleasant Villa. As neighbours there are Daisy Icchaporia, a violinist, and Villie Cardmaster, the Matka Queen – incidentally both unmarried ageing Parsi women. They have joined the league with Coomy and Miss.

Kutpitia in *Such a Long Journey.* Daisy Icchaporia used to play on the violin. It was her great wish to be able to play a solo concert. Rumour had it that she practiced playing the violin in the nude, like the great Paginini. She was therefore called Daisy-ninny behind her back. The soothing music from her violin acted like balm for the troubled soul of Nariman – it calmed him down on all those stressful occasions with unending nightmares. Villie Cardmaster is an ageing spinster and looks after her ageing parent. She also has the knack for dreaming numbers which would be the correct ones for the gambling game of Matka. She has some amount of fun in an otherwise lovely life by flirting (harmlessly) and gambling.

It would be appropriate to end this discussion on the Parsi environment in India with a few words about the quickly disappearing Parsi community. Commenting on this feature of the Parsi community, Nani Palkhivala says:

> "they will became a decadent community with a glorious past, a perilous present, and a dim future."[36]

This aspect rings true in Dr. Fitter's words, when Jal goes to enlist his help for his injured father:

> "Dr. Fitter secured the latch and went to grumble to Mrs. Fitter in the kitchen that Parsi men of today were useless, dithering idiots, the race had deteriorated. "When you think of our forefathers, the industrialists and shipbuilders who established the foundation of modern India, the philanthropists who gave us one hospitals and schools and libraries and baags, what luster they brought to our community and the nation. And this incompetent fellow cannot look after his father. Can't make a simple decision about taking him to hospital for an X-ray." [FM 51]

Misty's concern about his dwindling Parsi community is voiced in his interview with Dirk Bennett :

> "There are only 120,000 Parsees in the world. So it is not a threat or delusion that they are on the verge of disappearance. What is 60,000 in a city (Bombay) of 12 million ? And it is a pity when anything disappears from this world, any species, man, animal or insect." [37]

This genuine concern of Mistry is found in his creation of characters like Jal in *Family Matters* and Tehmul Lungraa in *Such a Larg Journey* . Both these characters are weak, indecisive, adult males, unmarried and more importantly, unassertive. They easily allow themselves to be ruled over.

Tehmul Lungraa is symbolically created as handicapped, needing help to get on with life, and after his fall from a tree in childhood, grew up into an adult with a child's mind. The character of Jal in *Family Matters* is drawn on similar lines. Older to Coomy by a couple of years, he allows himself to be ruled by her always and is generally weak and submissive. He has got impaired hearing and often fiddles with his hearing aid. Irritated at the sorry figure he cuts, Dr. Fitter comments:

> "... Is it any wonder they predict nothing but doom and gloom for the community? Demographics show we'll be extinct in fifty years. Maybe it's the best thing. What's the use of having spineless weaklings walking around, Parsi in name only." [FM 51]

Nusli, Alamai's nephew also belongs to this category. He is described as a 'boy-man', '*mua*-donkey', '*lumbasoo-baywakoof* and a 'boy-without-brain' and given to frequent bouts of giggling. He was like a son to Alamai and Dinshawji as they were childless. It seems Mistry has introduced Nusli just to emphasize the pathetic condition of the Parsi community. Gustad does not think highly of him either:

> "Nusli giggled as he offered his hand. He was skinny, and stood with stooped shoulders. A single – *paasri* weakling, thought Gustad as he shook the clammy hand, wondering how a vulture's sister could spawn a milquetoast like Nusli Perhaps it was inevitable." [SaLJ -240]

N.S. Dharan opines,

> "Rohinton Mistry, thus, records in his fiction the ethnic atrophy that has set in his community... The fate of his characters is interwoven with the fate of his community."[38]

This fact of alarmingly decreased number in the Parsi community is highlighted by the that Mistry's novels abound in characters who are adults,(male and female alike), either unmarried or widowed and leading an unhappy existence – Tehmul Lungraa, Miss Kutpitia in *Such a Long Journey,* Dina, Maneck, Fredoon in *A Fine Balance* and Coomy, Jal, Daisy Icchaporia, Villie Cardmaster in *Family Matters.* Says Aditi Kapoor on this theme:

> "Unless something is done to augment their fast depleting numbers and to revive their religion, the Parsis after an illustrious past could well just fade out in oblivion."[39]

REFERENCES

1. N.S. Dharan, 'Ethnic Atrophy Syndrome in Rohinton Mistry's Fiction', in Novy Kapadia, *Parsi Fiction* Vol. 2, New Delhi : Prestige Books, 2001.
2. Nilufer Bharucha, 'Why All This Pariness? An Assertion of Ethno-Religious Identity in Recent Novels written by Parsis', in Nilufer E. Bharucha and Vrinda Nabal, *Mapping Cultural Spaces : Postcolonial Indian Literature in English – Essays in Howour of Nissim Exkiel.* New Delhi: Vision Books Pvt. Ltd., 1998.
3. *Ibid.*
4. Twinkle Manavar, '*Rohimton Mistry's Such a Long Journey: A Thematic Study'* in Novy Kapadia, *Parsi Fiction* Vol. 2, New Delhi: Prestige Books, 2001.
5. V.L.V.N. Narendra Kumar, *Parsee Novel,* New Delhi: Prestige Books, 2002, p. 83.
6. Ali Lakhani, 'The Long Journey of Rohinton Mistry', Interview at the Vancouver International Writers' Festival, Publication Details not Available.
7. Meenakshi Mukherjee, *The Twice–Born Fiction,* New Delhi : Arnold Heinemann, 1972. pp. 132-133.
8. V.L.V.N. Narendra Kumar, *Parsee Novel,* New Delhi: Prestige Books, 2002, p. 80.
9. Geeta Doctor, "Long Day's Journey into the Light", *Literature Alive,* Vol. 4, No. 3 & Vol. 5, No. 1, p. 46.
10. Nilufer E. Bharucha, *Rohinton Mistry: Ethnic Enclosures and Transcultural Spaces,* Jaipur : Rawat Publications, 2003. p. 120.

11. Viney Kirpal, 'Post Modern Strategies in the Indian English Novel', *Litterit,* Vol. 22, No. 2, p. 26.
12. Interview Ali Lakhani.
13. Nilufer E. Bharucha, p. 127.
14. N.P. Sharma, 'Parsi Culture and Vision in Rohinton Mistry's *Such a Long Journey* and Firdous Kanga's *Trying to Grow* : A comparative Study 'in *The Fiction of Rohinton Mistry*: *Critical Studies,* ed. Jaydipsinh Dodiya, New Delhi: Prestige Books, 1998, p. 37.
15. V.L.V.N. Narendra Kumar, p. 16.
16. Avadhesh Kumar Singh, 'The Sense of Community in the Parsi Novels'. *The Literary Criterion* Vol. 32, No. 3, 1996.
17. Sudha P. Pandya, 'Narrating the Nation : Rewriting History in Meena Alexander's *Nampally Road* and Rohinton Mistry's *A Fine Balance'*, in Nory Kapdia, *Parsi Fiction,* Vol. 2, New Delhi: Prestige Books, 2001.
18. Savita Goel, 'A Literary Voyage to India: Rohinton Mistry's *A Fine Balance',* in Jasbir Jain, *Writers of Indian Diaspore*: *Theory and Practice,* Jaipur: Rawat Publications, 1998, pp. 197-198.
19. V.L.V.N. Narendra Kumar, p. 25.
20. *Ibid.* p. 21
21. Nilufer Bharucha, p. 148.
22. Angela Lambert, 'Touched with Fire', *The Guardian,* April 26, 2002.
23. Charu Chandra Mishra, 'Modes of Resistance in Rohinton Mistry's *Such a Long Journey',* in Novy Kapapia, *Parsi Fiction,* Vol. 2, New Delhi: Prestige Books, 2001, p. 7.
24. *Ibid.*
25. Nilufer E. Bharucha, pp. 33-34
26. V.L.V.N. Narendra Kumar, p. 20.
27. *Ibid.*
28. Peter Morey, *Fictions of India: Narrative and Power,* Edinburgh: Edinburgh Univ-Press, 2000, p. 184.
29. John Bemrose, 'Salaam Bombay: Rohinton Mistry Again Recreates his Birthplace', Maclean's April 22, 2002.
30. Sooni Taraporewala, *Men & Women, A Supplement of Sunday Times of India 13th July,2003.*
31. Nilufer E. Bharucha, p. 171.
32. *Ibid.* p. 172.

33. *Ibid*. p. 174.
34. V.L.V.N. Narendra Kumar, pp. 24-25.
35. Interview Ali Lakhani.
36. Nani Palkhivala, *We, the Nation: The Lost Decades*, New Delhi: UBS, 1994. p. 320.
37. Dirk Bennett,'Speaking Out', www.artsworld.com/books-film/new/rohinton mistry.
38. N.S. Dharan.
39. Aditi Kapoor, 'The Parsis; Fire on Ice,' *Times of India*, 14th May 1989.

3

Mistry's Bombay Trilogy

This chapter proposes to examine the various ways in which India in general, and Bombay in particular continues to engage Mistry's imagination and identify the varied moods and hues of the city as portrayed by him in his fictional work. Nilanjana S. Roy opines:

> "It was impossible to read *Family Matters* without being reminded repeatedly of the two other novels that preceded it, and I found it hard not to think to Mistry's three novels as a coherent entity. All three books follow the same essential structure, superimposing the tangled lives and concerns of their Parsi protagonists over an ongoing narrative of post – Indira India. All three are set in Bombay; or as in the case of *A Fine Balance*, in an unnamed city that bears such a strong resemblance to Bombay that the point is not worth quibbling about ... In brief, even though Mistry may not have intended to write his first three novels this way, they form a Bombay Trilogy."[1]

This part of the study, Mistry's Bombay Trilogy, traces the use of various Bombay metaphors, 'institutions' as depicted by Mistry in his three novels. In *Such a Long Journey,* Mistry discusses at length the various Bombay landmarks which he remembers prominently. Beginning with the Bhaiya, who supplies milk in the morning, the ubiquitous crow, the Bombay monsoon, Crawford market, Bhindi Bazar, Chor Bazar, Mount Mary Church etc. In *A Fine Balance* Mistry portrays yet another unexplored aspect of Bombay - the lives of the pavement dwellers, the slum dwellers and the middle class life of Bombay. In this novel the period used is that of the Internal Emergency imposed by the then Prime Minister Indira Gandhi. Mistry does not spare the readers any gory details of the life of the beggars. In *Family Matters*, Bombay as a city is idealized by Mr. Kapur who talks about it as an innocent girl, then a young woman and how the change of name to Mumbai will affect his comfortability. In the novel Inspector Masalawala comments,

> "To think that we Parsis were the ones who built this beautiful city and made it prosper. And in a few more years, there won't be any of us left alive to tell the tale."
>
> "Well, we are dying out, and Bombay is dying as well," said Dr. Fitter. "When the spirit departs, it isn't long before the body decays and disintegrates." [Family Matters-416]

Such a Long Journey (1991), Mistry's first novel revolves around a Parsi family of Bombay. The protagonist Gustad Noble works as a bank clerk in the metropolis of Bombay – it was Mistry's vocation too in Toronto when he migrated from Bombay. The novel begins with a very calm, early morning scene, with Gustad getting ready to offer prayers to Ahura Mazda, facing eastwards. The serenity of the scene is disturbed by the clatter of pots and pans brought out by women of Khodadad building for their daily quota of milk being dispensed by the *bhaiya.* It is left to the readers to decipher that *bhaiya* is actually the word used by Bombayites for milkman – Mistry does not bother to clarify though.

> "Doors opened and slammed shut, money jingled, a voice called out with special instructions for the *bhaiya's* next delivery. Someone joked with the man: *'Arre' bhaiya*, why not sell the milk and water separately ? Better for the customer, easier for you also – no mining to do. 'This was followed by the bhaiya's usual impassioned denial." [SaLJ-5]

The early morning hour also signaled one of the busiest of the day for Dilnavaz, as she had to fill up the various vessels with water for the day's use, failing which the family's daily needs could not be fulfilled. This refers to Bombay's water problem, a perpetual one owing to the limited water resources and a population which is always on the increase.

> "For Dilnavaz, that familiar hissing, spitting, blustering was a summons to waken." [SaLJ-5] "She went to the bathroom and connected the transparent plastic hose to fill the water drums, even though today there was time enough to brush her teeth first, and make tea. It was five o'clock – two whole hours before the taps went dry." [SaLJ-7].

The first chapter ends on an uneasy note for Gustad as he finds a notice from the Bombay Municipal Corporation struck on the wall surrounding Khodadad building, which simply states the government's intention to pull down the wall to widen the road.

In the second chapter Gustad plans a visit to the well known Crawford Market of Bombay in order to get a live chicken to celebrate his daughter, Roshan's birthday. Mistry takes the reader on an extensively guided tour of the wholesale and retail vegetable, fruit and meat market located in south Bombay, which can well lay claim to being one of its landmarks. Fondly reminiscing of happy childhood days, filled with abundance, Gustad was in the habit of accompanying his father to Crawford Market to buy live chickens. They used to travel by taxi, usually with a servant in tow. However, Gustad's limited means did not allow for such luxuries. He traveled by bus, with a worn out basket lined with newspaper to absorb meat juices, and a constant fear of offending fellow passengers in the bus. He did not look forward to his visits to Crawford Market.

> "For Gustad, Crawford Market had no charms. It was a dirty, smelly, overcrowded place where the floors were slippery with animal ooze and vegetable was to, where the cavernous hall of meat was dark and for bidding, with huge, wicked – looking meat hooks hanging from the ceiling ... and the

constant, sinister flash of a meat cleaver or butcher's knife which, more often than not, was brandished in the vendor's wild hand as he bargained and gesticulated." [SaLJ-21].

Along with Crawford Market, Mistry brings in the character of Malcolm Saldanha, a Goan Christian, and Gustad's friend, who teaches him the benefits of eating beef in a Hindu dominated country and also guides him in selecting the choicest parts. Here is Mistry's chance of introducing another Bombay institution, the Royal School of Music and Trinity College, where students taught by Malcolm's father to play violin and piano, periodically took examinations.

"Malcolm's mother played first violin with the Bombay Chamber Orchestra, and his elder brother, the oboe." [SaLJ-23).]

Although Mistry does not welcome questions pertaining to autobiographical elements in his work, it is certainly worth mentioning that Sohrab, in *Such A Long Journey* and Murad and Jehangir in *Family Matters* study in the prestigious St. Xavier's High School of Bombay, Mistry's alma mater too. It was to celebrate Sohrab's admission and first day of School that Gustad decides to give him a treat with lunch at the Parisian and pistachio ice-cream at K. Rustom & Co. While going to Churchgate, they get on the wrong bus and are ordered out of the bus by a rude conductor in the middle of the traffic with Gustad, meeting with an accident in an attempt to save his son. The alert people of Bombay immediately crowded around him and made him as comfortable as the situation would permit. A resourceful taxi driver ordered his passengers out and rushed Gustad and Sohrab home. Once there, Major Bilimoria decided that the best course of treatment would be at Madhiwalla Bonesetter's with his alternative methods of treatment. Nilufer Bharucha opines".

"This provides Mistry with the opportunity ofevoking yet another old Bombay institution, the traditional bone setter Dr. Madhiwalla. The skills of Madhiwalla and now his descendents are fervently sworn to by generations of Bombayites, Parsi and non-Parsi."[2]

Lunchtime of the bank offers Mistry the opportunity to invoke the incredible *dubbawallas* of Bombay. The *dubbawalla's* job is to collect lunch packed in tiffin boxes from the respective homes of the clients, deliver them atf the place of work, again collect the empty boxes at the appropriate time, and return it to their homes. And all this is done with amazing synchronization, with the *dubbawallas* traveling in local trains, and never does a dubba reach the wrong destination.

It would be interesting to mention at this point the fact that so impressed was Prince Charles with the institution of dubbawallas, on his last visit to India, that invitations were promptly issued to two of them to enable them to attend his wedding with Camilla Parker Bowles in London!

> "They emerged under the hot sun, stepping out of the path of a tardy *dubbawalla* weaving through the crowds at a joy, his crateof lunch – boxes balanced on his head. A gust of wind picked up the sweat streaming down his face and sent it in their direction." [Sal J-72].

The next institution of Bombay invoked by Mistry is the Chor Bazar, which had obvious negative connotations in the yesteryears as suggested by the name, but does not answer to any of those at present. Major Jimmy Bilimoria enlists Gustad's help in the top secret government assignment he is currently involved in. He instructs Gustad, vide a letter to undertake a visit to Chor Bazar, where he would be met by the contact man. It will be appropriate to quote an interesting exchange between Gustad and his wife Dilnavaz in this connection:

> "Why Chor Bazar ? That's not a nice place." "Don't be silly. Because the old name is still used doesn't mean it's full of thieves. Even Foreign tourists go there nowadays." [SaLJ-92].

Dilnavaz's words echo the negative vibes associated with Chor Bazar. Gustad, however does not share her fears and rather looks forward to his visit, having arranged for a half day off from his bank. The visit revives memories of his childhood when he used to accompany his father to Chor Bazar to buy various things - his Meccano set had been bought after much bargaining, and he had used it to create models of a fire – engine, crane, racing car, steamboat, etc. Gustad took his time, leisurely looking around the various wares on sale:

> "He handed back the set, ran a hand through his hair and surveyed the series of lanes running perpendicular to the main road, all littered with a miscellany of goods, as though a convoy of lorries had symmetrically spilled their loads. Much of it was metal glass, gleaming in the hot afternoon sun. Worthless junk lay side by side with valuable objects : Chipped cups and saucers, Meissen were, Sheffield cutlery, vases, brass lamps, Limoges percelain, solder – repaired cooking utensils ewers, ... Umbrellas, crystal wineglasses." [SaLJ-100-01]

Other interesting sights that met his eye included an earwax remover who performed his task with the help of a 'slender silver instrument'; a masseur who was very keen to give Gustad either a 'head *maalis* or a foot *maalis*; a busy pavement barber; and several books stalls with titles both in Hindi and English. At one such stall Gustad selected three volumes paying six rupees, to adorn the book case he intended to make with Sohrab in the future. At another book stall he comes across the volume entitled. The *Complete Works of William Shakespeare,* bound in read cloth with the title in gold lettering, just as Major Bilimoria had indicated in the letter. The stall owner turns out to be Ghulam Mohammed, the same taxi driver, and at present an undercover colleague of the Major, who had been instrumental in saving Gustad's life many years ago, when the latter had had a nasty fall while getting down from a bus in the middle of a lot of traffic.

The next meeting with Ghulam Mohammed takes Gustad to the Red Light area of Bombay, referred to as the House of Cages by Mistry, taking the opportunity to comment on another un-ignorable aspect of Bombay. The locality was familiar to Gustad as their family physician; Dr. Paymaster had his clinic there. Outside the prostitute's quarters there was a stall of

Peerbhoy Paanwalla, who reveled in narrating erotic stories about the exploits of clients who visited the women.

> "The House of Cages offered a full range of services, from the brisk, no-nonsense hand job even the poorest of day labourers could offered, to the most intricate contortions from a standard *Kama-Sutra* or *The Parfumed Garden.* Something to suit the tumescence of every customer and wallet." [SaLJ-157]

Along with the House of Cages Mistry does not fail to mention Bhindi Bazaar of Bombay, famous for its scented oils and perfumes.

After getting the package containing ten lakh rupees home, Gustad debates for several days on the various possibilities of depositing the money with the bank he works in. This inordinate delay invites the displeasure of Ghulam Mohammed who plants first a headless bandicoot and then a headless cat in the Vinca bushes outside Gustad's flat. All this happens in the monsoon season.

> "Around midnight the rain commenced. He heard the first drops chime against the panes. By the time he got to the window the rain become a downpour. The wind was sweeping it inside. He took a deep breath to savour the fresh moist earth fragrance, feeling great satisfaction. as though he had had a hand in t he arrival of the monsoon. It will be good for my vinca bush." [SaLJ-129]

Bharucha feels Mistry could recall the monsoon in a nostalgic vein.

> "Gustad's work for his old friend takes place against the ominous backdrop of the breaking of the Bombay monsoon, yet another Bombay familiarity that Mistry would definitely have recalled with nostalgia or irritation (for the inconveniences it causes in flooded roads) in Canada[3]

The dead bodies of the bandicoot and cat in the vinca bush attract a lot of crows with the breaking of day. It is the persistent cawing of the crows that attract Gustad's attention to the dead bodies.

> "Crows had gathered from miles around. Besides the multitude teeming in the compound; there were clusters on the entrance steps, shaking out water from their feathers. Another disciplined black line perched along the awning. The crows waited, wandering if they were about to lose their banquet." [SaLJ-133].

A reader not familiar with Bombay might wonders why a lot of space is ascribed to description of the black feathered multitudes, but one familiar to the sights and sounds of Bombay like Mistry is would think that the crows of Bombay also find a just representation in Mistry's first novel. The discovery of the brutally butchered bodies of the bandicoot and cat summon the services of the guard on duty of night – the Gurkha.

> "The Gurkha was a small, bow-legged man whose calf muscles bulged powerfully, as did the sinews of his forearms... He had not yet changed out of his uniform : Khaki shirt and Khaki short pants, with a Kaki cap. Round his waist was the leather belt carrying the ceremonial Gurkha Kukri : a short broad – bladed sword, and nestling near the Lilt, two tiny daggers in their separate sheaths." [SaLJ-135].

Bharucha's comments on the Gurkha in this context are quite pertinent:

> "The Gurkha of course is/was yet another Bombay speciality – The tough Nepalian – serviceman who would eke out his army pension by working as a watchman for residential complexes in Bombay. The bravery of the Gurkha soldier in war and his legendary loyalty made him an ideal watchdog in an increasingly crime ridden city. However, this once the Gurkha was not of much use to Khodadad Building..."[4]

At this juncture, everything in Gustad's life seems to be going wrong – he is not in control of things anymore. The reins of his life seem to have been wrenched out by a power which is in control of everyone's destiny. Roshan's illness, which had earlier shown signs of improvement, aggravates further, with the doctor suggesting hospitalization for better treatment; Dinshawji's health suddenly deteriorates, making it clear that his outward jovial nature was actually a camouflage for the intense pain (both physical and other wise) that he endured at all times – his remarks to Gustad is very poignant:

> "Let me tell you, it's more difficult to be a jovial person all the time than to be a quiet, sickly one." The truth of Dinshawji's words was sharp and cruel. [SaLJ-180].

Almost half the money having already been deposited in the bank with Dinshawji's help, Major Bilimoria's sudden arrest in New Delhi necessitates it to be withdrawn again at double speed, to be sent back to Delhi. Tragedy strikes the day after Dinshawji completes the transaction. He collapsed in office and had to be rushed to the Parsi General hospital. His condition gradually worsens as does Roshan's and it is at this critical juncture that Gustad's Goan Christian friend, Malcolm is brought back into the narrative. Malcolm elaborates upon the miracles of asking Mother Mary of the Church of Mount Mary for help. Over the next few pages Mistry informs readers of this important landmark of Bombay, how to reach the place and the procedure followed thereafter. Mistry also talks about the local trains of Bombay, describing the sea of humanity getting in and out of the fast moving trains, stopping at stations for a few seconds.

> "At two o'clock, a fast train to Virar pulled into Grant Road station. The surging, jostling exchange of bodies commenced, then the train pulled out: the over flowing third class; the cushioned first class; the Ladies only, windows covered with special metal grills, with chinks so tiny, not one molesting, eve-teasing finger could poke through. On the platform, the sign changed to show the next arrival ... In a few minutes, at Bombay central, the two were able to get window seats. ... Gustad read the station names as the blue, white and red signs on the platforms periodically swept past his window. Mahalaxmi. Lower Parel. Elphinstone Road. Dadar ... Matunga station... The train passed over Mahim Creek, and the stink of raw sewage mingled with salty sea smells made them wrinkle their noses.... "Next one is Bandra." [SaLJ – 223, 24].

The readers is left wondering, are Gustad and Malcolm taking the local train to Bandra or is it Mistry reminiscing about the life he has left behind, rattling off names of stations on a particular routc. (onc after the other). More information waits the reader once they reach the Church. The reader along with Gustad is justifiably surprised at the array awaiting his eyes :

> "Arranged in neat rows were fingers, thumbs, hands, elbows, arms (inclusive of fingers), kneecaps, feet, things and truncated bys. The hands and feet came in left and right, in two sizes : child and adult. Skulls, eyes, noses, ears, and lips were grouped separately from limbs and digits. Complete male and female wax figures were also available". [SaLJ-226].

Malcolm explained to Gustad how people suffering from an ailment came to Mother Mary and offered the troublesome body part in wax to her, she was 'the Mechanic for all sufferers'. Under Malcolm's guidance Gustad prayed for Roshan, Dinshawji and Sohrab. After prayers at the Church were over, the two friends spent some time on the rocky sea beach of Bandra, remembering old times.

Khodadad Building is surrounded by a wall which unfortunately is used as a public lavatory at night much to the annoyance of the inhabitants. A pavement artist is engaged by Gustad to paint portraits of gods and goddesses on the wall, in order to stop the malpractices of the people and stop the malodour arising thereby.

> "Over the next few days, the wall filled up with goods, prophets and saints. When Gustad checked the air each morning and evening, he found it free of malodours. Mosquitoes and flies were no longer quite the nuisance they used to be; with their breeding grounds drying up, thenumbers diminished dramatically." [SaLJ-183]

Gustad although being a Parsi encourages the pavement artist to portray as many religions as he can, and the latter complies with.

> "Nataraja did his cosmic dance, Abraham lifted his are high above Isaac, Mary cradled the Infant Jesus, Laxmi dispensed wealth, Saraswati Spread wisdom and learning." [SaLJ- 184].

This attitude of Gustad (Mistry's) is in keeping with the Parsi worldview of religious tolerance but Nilufer Bhamcha feels this is an attitude typical of Bombay:

> "So, the wall of all Religions comes into existence and re-affirms Bombay's famed tolerance in the face of increased fundamentalism violence... uncertain being the key word for Bombay's minorities, religions and linguistic in a city in the clutches of a political and criminal mafia."[5]

But the solace provided by the wall to the inhabitants of Khodadad Building seems to be temporary, as Malcolm, ironically enough, in his official capacity as an employee of the Municipal Corporation arrives with his contingent to demolish this very wall. However, once there, he meets with stiff resistance from a *morcha* (Mistry's bag of Bombay specials is yet to be empty). The morcha consists of Dr. Paymaster and Peerbhoy Paanwalla at the head of the procession and has representation from all sections of society – they have come together to protest against the high handed behaviour of the Municipal Corporation.

Malcolm hailed from a family of musicians, his father was very good with the violin, his mother also played the violin, his elder brother played the oboe and he played the piano. He dreamt of being a professional musician, but for the sake of a steady income, had taken up the present job with the municipality, using his uncle's influence. He was however not happy with the state of things:

> "This bloody city, turning into a harsh, merciless place. No bloody security with piano tuitions, no telling when students could vanish ... And the beautiful music was gradually disappearing too, as surely as discipline. It was like watching the slow death of a loved one. Thank god for the Time and Talents club, ... for the Max Mueller Bhavan, for the British

council, for the GDR Cultural Centre, for the USIS. Or the music would have died a long time ago. But ... the golden age of western classical music in this city was definitely over." [SaLJ-319].

In Malcolm's mourning the 'erosion of beautiful music from Bombay' Bharucha feels "Mistry's own limitations vis-à-vis music of the Indian type which is well and alive in the city of Bombay" is revealed. Bharucha pulls up Mistry for "such a definition of 'culture' which could also be called an instance of a colonial mind set that has survived the end of empire."[6]

Another point worth mentioning here is the discussion/ argument that takes place between Dinshawji and Gustad on the matter of changing/renaming various roads, streets and squares. Gustad taking a tolerant stand finds nothing wrong in it if it keeps the authorities (Marathas) happy. Dinshawji, however, is much agitated and believes in the permanency of things and feels a sense of insecurity.

"Why change the names ? ... Hutatma chowk ! ... What is wrong with Flora Fountain ? ... No, Gustad ... you are wrong. Names are so important. I grew up on Lamingten Road. But it has disappeared, in its place is Dadasaheb Bhadkhamkar Marg. My school was on Carnac Road. Now suddenly it's on Lokmanya Tilak Marg. I live at Sleater Road, soon that will also disappear. My whole life I have come to work at flora fountain. So what happens to the life I have lived ? was I living the wrong life, with all the wrong names ? Will I get a second chance to live if all again, with these new names ? Tell me what happens to my life. Rubbed out, just like that ? Tell me !" [SaLJ-73, 74].

David Williams explains Dinshawji's predicament as,

"Though Dinshawji laments a wholesale loss of connections, including the loss of his social identity and even his personal history, the erasure of the old names also removes the world for him, makes absent what should be 'naturally' present ultimately, he experiences the rewriting of the map of his neighbourhood as an interruption in his self-presence. And so, to him, a life by any other name could not be the same life."[7]

The disagreement of Gustad and Dinshawji on the subject of changing names almost seems like Mistry trying to resolve within himself as to what should be acceptable. The Bombay he was born and brought up in, and so accurately portrays in his fiction has became Mumbai. It seems the writer is aware of the inevitability of things, but still finds it quite difficult to accept at face value. In his review of *such a Long Journey*, Bharucha comments:

> "From the vantage point of the 1990s Mistry has reviewed the remembered past, the decades of the 1960s and 70s, when the ills that beset Bombay today, first began to manifest themselves. Recalling those decades when Bombay, before she became Mumbai, began to fall from grace, Mistry has pulled out all the stops and evoked all the real and apocryphal Bombay specials, which makes this novel a quintessential Bombay book."[8]

Mistry's second novel, *A Fine Balance* also won a string of literary awards. As has already been noted, this one too deals with India. In his second novel Mistry has widened his canvas somewhat and the reader gets to know not only the 'City by the Sea' (Bombay, of course), but travels with the author to gather more information about the lives of Ishvar and Om Prakesh Darji to a 'village by a River's and with Maneck Kohlah to the 'Mountains'. Sudha Pandya writes.

> "Homelessness is not all about crippling nostalgia and writers sometimes use their location as an enabling creative exercise to create a literacy space, or to forge a living link with their past ... And so he continues to write about India, about Bombay, about Parsisand other minority communities."[9]

The novel, spanning over 700 pages, is set between a 'Prologue: 1975 '(the imposition of Internal Emergency by Indira Gandhi) and an 'Epilogue : 1984' (the assassination of Indira Gandhi by her Sikh body guards). Before the Prologue, however, is a quotation from Balzac, which sets the tone and prepares the reader for what is to follow:

> "Holding this book in your hand, sinking back in your soft armchair, you will say to yourself perhaps it will amuse me. And after your have read this story of great misfortunes, you will no doubt dine well, blaming the author for your own insensitivity, accusing him of wild exaggeration and flights of fancy. But rest assured : this tragedy is not a fiction. All is true.
> Honore de Balzac, *Le Pire Goriot*"[AFB].

What the reader is not prepared for, however, is the grim tale that gradually unfolds before her eyes. Here is a Bombay painted in very dark and sinister shades and quite surprising after one has gone through *Such a Long Journey*, where the author's tone is more of fond reminiscence – going all out to record the sights and sounds of Bombay,visiting the landmarks down memory lane. The picture of Bombay in a Fine Balance is very dismal. Mistry finds "Bombay very oppressive and overcrowded"[10]

In an interview with Geoff Hancock, Mistry has gone on record to say that he found Bombay to be grim and depressing:"Bleak wasthe picture I created when I was here. That's exactly the way it is"[11]

The novel begins with the portrayal of a scene on an overcrowded local train of Bombay, with passengers literally hanging out, but not losing the 'fine balance'.

> "The Morning Express bloated with passengers slowed to a crawl, then lurched forward suddenly, as though to resume full speed. The train's brief deception jolted its riders. The bulge of humans hanging out of the doorway distended perilously, like a soap bubble at its limit." [AFB - 3].

The scene mentioned above addresses typical problems of Bombay – an ever burgeoning population, with not enough amenities to meet the demand, which results in scenes like this. People board the train, pushed by the crowd and the same crowd pressure pushes them out at stations when they want to get down. Mistry introduces three of the four protagonists in the following two paragraphs. Maneck Kohlah who was standing in the compartment, "held on to the overhead railing, propped up securely within the crush." [AFB-3].

When the train had a brief jolt Maneck's textbooks fell out of his hand upon the back of Omprakash Darji, who had been catapulted into the arms of his uncle, Ishvar Darji. With the usual round of apologies over, the passengers impatiently wait for the train to start after its unscheduled halt. Omprakash looked out of the window to try and identify where:

> "Rough shacks stood beyond the railroad fence, alongside a ditch running with raw sewage. Children were playing a game with sticks and stones. An excited puppy danced around them, trying to join in. Nearby, a shirtless man was milking a cow. They could have been anywhere. The acrid smell of a lung-fire drifted towards the train." [AFB – 4].

The scene that meets Om's eye on looking out of the window could belong anywhere in India, but the surprising fact is that the protagonists are on a local train in Bombay, traveling within city limits and the fact remains that 'raw sewage', 'a shirtless man milking a cow' and 'acrid smell of dung-fire' are all part of the cosmopolitan fabric of Bombay. The next scene on the agenda is a vendor of combs, who has somehow managed to push his way through the jam-packed passengers.

> "Plastic hairband, unbreakable, plastic hairclip, flower shape, butterfly shape, colourful comb, unbreakable. The comb seller recited in a halfhearted monotone ... Big comb and small comb, pink, orange, maroon, green, blue, yellow comb – unbreakable." [AFB - 5].

This is yet another commonality of the local trains in Bombay where much business is transacted by vendors ... selling various kinds of things elbowing and jostling through the crowds, mostly cheap, inviting animosity of the passengers who are not interested in buying these items.

The passengers soon discover the reason for the train's sudden and long halt – a dead body has been found on the rail tracks.

> "The men who had wandered outside came back with news that yet another body had been found by the tracks, near the level crossing. Maneck edged towards the door to listen. A nice, quick way to go, he thought, as long as the train had struck the person squarely ... why does everybody have to choose the railway tracks only for dying ? grumbled another. No consideration for people like us. Murder, suicide, Naxalite – terrorist killing, police – custody death – everything ends up delaying the trains. What is wrong with poison or tall buildings or knives ?" [AFB-6].

The words 'yet another body' having been found on the tracks suggest the alarming frequency with which it happens and equally alarming are the people's reaction. While Maneck considers it to be a very effective way to die-a kind of touch and go situation, also one which has the future potential of his committing suicide on one such track towards the end of the novel :

> "When the first compartment had entered the station, he stepped off the platform and on to the gleaming silver tracks ... Maneck's last thought was that he still had Avinash's chessmen." [AFB - 749].

Maneck's thoughts on committing suicide on the railway tracks in the Prologue leave the readers with a sense of foreboding which unfortunately bears fruit in the Epilogue. The reaction of the other passengers to the dead body found on the tracks is so matter-of fact that one is left wondering, does a death by suicide on the railway tracks in a big city like Bombay merit no more sympathy than mere annoyance at the inordinate delay in reaching destinations. Or does it point towards other larger issues, like some deaths among the teeming millions of Bombay are hardly enough to cause a flutter among the survivors? Are people so used to such unhappy endings that they do not bother to ask why, or who, but just accept it, brush it aside like rubbish and move on? Though this one episode Mistry seems to be pointing to these and other issues that really make a difference to the general public of Bombay.

After the dead body is removed by the authorities, the train moves on, reaches the station where the tailors, Ishvar and Omprakash Darji want to get down, and so does Maneck. It turns out that all three of them are looking for the same person-Dina Dalal, the tailors for work, and Maneck for paying guest accommodation. Incidentally, Dina Dalal, completes the pictures of the foursome, around whom the novel revolves. On the way to her flat, outside the station, they come across a beggar – part of an important institution of Bombay, which Mistry addresses in quite some details in the novel.

They passed a beggar slumped upon a small wooden platform fitted with castors, which raised him four inches off the ground. His fingers and thumbs were missing, and his legs were amputated almost to the buttocks. 'O babu, ek paisa day-ray ! 'he song, shaking a tin can between his bandaged palms. 'O babu ! Hai babu! Aray babu, ek paisa day-ray!'

> 'That's one of the worst I've seen since coming to the city,' said Ishvar, and the others agreed. [AFB – 7,8].

The beggar in question here, is called Shankar – the very act of providing a beggar with a name, speaks volumes to the discerning reader about the authorial intention. The introduction of the said Shankar and Ishvar's poignant comment that he (Shankar) was one of the worst he had seen in the city only serves to confirm the fact that beggars are to seen in abundance in Bombay. As the story progresses, the reader is introduced to Beggarmaster, who calls Shankar 'worm' after his appearance (in fact, that's what he is called, the tailors not withstanding). Beggarmaster is created in the Dickensian shades of Fagin, but somewhat some shades too dark and grim. He proclaims grandly:

> 'Usually, when I look after a beggar, I charge one hundred rupees per week. That includes begging space, food, clothes, and protection. Also, special things like bandages or crutches... I am the most famous Beggar master in the city. Naturally, the Facilitator contacted me. Anyway, your case is different, you don't need looking after in the same

way. Besides, you've been good to worm. Just pay me fifty a week per person, for one year. That will be enough.' [AFB – 449].

The tailors had been picked off the street one night, along with other beggars, under the city Beautification programme. Sergeant Kesar and his constables were ordered to pick up the pavement dwellers and dump them in waste land outside the city, as a solution to the beggary problem. After some time they come up with a better idea and send them to a labour camp to work on an irrigation project, thus saving on the expenses of skilled labour. So Ishvar and Om had landed up at the labour camp, from where they had been 'bought' back by the Beggar-master, and he had promised to 'look' after them in return for some money. The vicious circle seems to be complete here. But the ease with which Shankar describes the horrors of his profession, has readers surely squirming in their seats in the comfort of their homes.

"Also, Beggar-master has to be very imaginative. If all beggars have the same injury, public gets used to it and feels no pity. Public likes to see variety. Some wounds are so common, they don't work anymore. For example, putting out a baby's eyes will not automatically earn money. Blind beggars are everywhere. But blind, with eyeballs missing, face showing empty sockets, plus nose chopped off – now anyone will give money for that. Diseases are also powerful. A big growth on the neck or face, oozing yellow, pus. That works well.' [AFB - 403].

The matter-of-fact attitude Shankar exudes makes readers marvel at his all-out-acceptance of his fate. He does not complain, even in his state with no fingers, no feet, no legs, propelling himself around on his platform with wheels, with the help of his palms. Mistry hides nothing of the grotesqueness that is rampant in the begging profession, bent upon recording every gory detail that the reader might not be aware of that also exists side by side with the skyscrapers in the city of Bombay. Beggar-master is akin to a one-man industry, creating novel injuries and mutilations, ensuring that wounds stay 'nicely' festered and unhealed, reserving a particular place for every beggar under his care, guaranteeing that no further misfortune would befall them – so many services provided for a mere hundred rupees per week per beggar. Savita Goel compares this to Meera Nair's *Salaam Bombay*:

> "Mistry's authentic portrayal of Bombay and its social ills such as child labour and beggary problem bears a close affinity to Meera Nair's film *Salaam Bombay*. The description of the beggar-master with his imaginative mind, training his beggars and dressing them with a variety of wounds manages to raise a laugh as their chill penury is juxtaposed with the lighter side of their lives."[12]

The next issue raised by Mistry in the Prologue regarding Bombay is the fact that it is regarded by many as a city of many opportunities, a place where one comes to from one's native place to earn lots of money and ultimately hopes to go back to one's native place, once the purpose is accomplished.

Maneck said he hated it here, and could not wait to return to his home in the mountains, next year, when he finished college.

> 'We have also come for a short time only.' said Ishvar. 'To earn some money, then go back to our village. What is the use of such a big city ? Noise and crowds, no place to live, water scarce, garbage everywhere. Terrible.' [AFB - 8].

The tailors had been born in the lowly Chamaar caste in 'a village by a river' where their family had suffered untold of tortures at the hands of the upper caste Thakurs and Brahmins. Ishvar's father, Dukhi Mochi, tortured by the high handedness of theupper caster, dreamt of a better life for his sons, Ishvar and Narayan. At a very early age they were apprenticed to his friend Ashraf, who worked as a tailor in the city. Having learnt the skill of tailoring, they were soon able to free the family from a hand-to-mouth existence. In due course, Narayan married and Omprakash was born. Ishvar and Om lived with Ashraf Chacha in the city helping him and also earning money at tailoring. Meanwhile, Narayan tried a revolution of sorts by daring to insist on casting his own vote. As punishment, he was flogged and burnt and his entire family set on fire. Business at the small town having got scarce, they decided to try their luck in the city of dreams and opportunities – Bombay. Maneck, too was sent by his father from the hill station which housed their small general stores, to get a technical education so that he could come back with better ideas and education for a better and brighter future. So Maneck comes to Bombay but is already depressed and dejected by what he sees. Rajaram, the hair collector, who befriends them, echoes their sentiments, their hopes and their yet unvoiced, worst fears.

> 'Yes, thousands and thousands are coming to the city because of bad times in their native place. I came for the same reason.'
>
> 'But we don't want to stay long.' 'Nobody does,' said Rajaram. 'who wants to live like this ?' His hand moved in a tired semicircle, taking in the squalid hutments, the ragged field, the huge slum across the road wearing its malodorous crown of cooking smoke and industrial effluvium. 'But some, times people have no choice. Sometimes the city grabs you, sinks its claws into you, and refuses to let go.' [AFB - 209].

Rajaram's fears, are aptly explained by Savita Goel,

> Depressed and demoralized by the ruthless murder of their entire family, pressured by joblessness and hunger and envisioning a bright future for themselves, Ishvar and Omprakash migrate to Bombay like Rajaram ... Their lives in Bombay symbolize the anguish, pain, anxiety and restlessness of people cut off fromtheir native village ... Their incapacity to find a home, despite numerous efforts is touching and pitiable. They are caught in an inescapable dilemma, between two worlds – their native village which they abandoned because it held a bleak chance and Bombay which has failed them despite promises – they stay on as marginal men, unable to discard the old and to find peace in the new.[13]

When work gets inadequate at Ashraf Chacha's shop, the tailors decide to try their luck in the big city of Bombay. Arriving by train, with Nawaz's address, (got from Ashraf),

> 'Ishvar and Omprakash stood frozen on the edge of the Commotion ... what a huge crowd ... He took the trunk, struggling urgently against the barrier of bodies and luggage, as though assured that once they were past it, everything would be all right – the city of promise lay beyond this final obstacle.' [AFB - 186].

Arriving in Bombay at night, they are horrified to find that the footpaths were covered with sleeping people, who resembled dead bodies in their recovered stillness. More shocks await them at Nawaz's house, where he (Nawaz) refuses to acknowledge the fact that he had received a letter from Ashraf, informing him of their arrival. After much cajoling and many denials, he very 'grudgingly agreed to let them sleep under the awning behind the kitchen for a few days, till they found accommodation. 'I do this for no one but. Ashraf,' he emphasized. 'The thing is, there is hardly room here for my own family. [AFB - 187].

Nawaz does not offer them any dinner, either, nor is there any tea forth coming the next morning or any morning of their stay, for that matter. The only one occasion that they are offered tea and dinner at Nawaz's is when a separate accommodation and work as tailors for Dina Dalal are found for them. Hailing form a village as they do, the tailors are at first shocked of the hostility displayed by Nawaz, but quickly attribute the feature to the pressures of the city. When Om grumbles about this fact, his uncle wisely answers:

> 'All people are not the same. Besides, Nawaz's years in the city must have altered him. Places can change people, you know. For better or worse.' [AFB - 190].

The problem of accommodation does seem to be a grave and genuine one in Bombay. If there is a beggar-master, there should logically be a slumlord. So Mistry creates one

"A slumlord called Thokray, who controls everything in this area – country liquor, hashish, hung. And when there are riots, he decides who gets burned and who survives.' [AFB - 198]

So the tailors, six months after their arrival in the city, take up accommodation in a slum – a house whose mud floor was partially covered with planks, with a patch work of plywood and sheet metal making up the walls. The roof consisted of a sheet of old corrugated iron with corroded areas being covered with transparent plastic. For water they would be required to use the common tap in the middle of the lane and the railway tracks running beside were to suffice for toilets. A hundred rupees a month was the rent to be paid, always in advance. At the slum they meet other minor characters who have some significance in the development of the novel; Rajaram the hair collector, who changes a variety of professions, from barber to hair collector_to motivator for the family planning programme, even commits the murder of two beggars in order to acquire their hair, and as the novel draws to an end, we see him in the role of Bal Baba, the sanyasi, predicting the future for the hapless millions – this for a person who is uncertain of his own future. There is also character of Monkey Man, who owns a couple of monkeys, named Laila and Majnoo, and a dog, Tikka, whom he uses to regale audience with monkey tricks. Tragedy strikes his life when the dog kills the two monkeys when all three animals are shut up in the room for the entire day, because the slum dwellers are forcibly taken to attend a public meeting of the Prime Minister, Mrs. Indira Gandhi. Monkey Man, in anger, kills his dog and now takes to showing juggling and balancing acts with his sisters two children, the children tied to a long pole, raised high, balanced on his thumb – the picture of fine balance that appears on the cover of *A Fine Balance.* There are also the sorcerer Dayaram, the Harmonium-player and the old woman who 'could' read entrails as fluently as a swami could read the Bhagvad Gita'. [AFB – 332].

Bharucha finds the portrayal of characters here like the celebrated Raj Kapoor film *Shri 420*

> In passages redolent of an almost socialist nostalgia perhaps engendered by the memories of boyhood viewings of the 1950's film *Shri 420*, Raj Kapoor's socialist epic, Mistry has the tailors sitting outside their hut in the evening listening to the harmonium player as he plays his instrument and sings old Hindi film song, in a rather idealised poor man's camaraderie.[14]

Mistry does nothing to tone down his language while describing the life at the slums. A large number of people living below the poverty line, trying their level best to make both ends meet, but still, a wide void left gaping, which nobody tries to reduce. A pathetic picture of the squalor and poverty of people at the slums is presented by Mistry with all the gory details – the reader is spared nothing.

Outside the platform, a woman sat in the sun with a small basket of vegetables beside her. She was drying her laundered sari, one half at a time. One end was wound wet round her waist and over her shrunken breasts, as far as it would go. The drying half was stretched along the railway fence, flowing from her body like a prayer in the evening sun. She waved to Om as the two passed by.

> 'She lives in our colony, 'he said ... 'She sells vegetables. She has only one sari.' [AFB - 348].

Gandhian principles advocating a simple life, say a person should be satisfied with two sets of clothes – one to wear and the other to wash and keep for the next day. What advice would one give to such people as the old vegetable vendor mentioned above who possess only one sari, which is washed and dried on the human body. Savita Goel opines:

> The writer presents a cross – section of Bombay – the huge slum across the road wearing its malodorous crown of cooking smoke and industrial effluvium, the long queue for water, accompanied by quarrels, lack of basic amenities,

open air toilets, the familiar sights of beggars with their begging bowls and the beggar master paying the police every week to avoid harassment.

At the slum where Ishvar and Om rent a room there is only one tap which runs in the morning, where long queues and quarrels are a common sight. Om is not aware and is rebuked by an old woman:

> 'Don't you know ?' the woman called. 'It only runs in the morning.'... 'Water only comes in the morning,' she repeated. 'Are you planning to wait by the tap till dawn ?' Opening the lid of a round-bottomed earthen matka, she transferred two glassfuls into his copper pot. 'Remember, you have to fill up early. Wake up late, and you go thirsty. Like the sun and moon, water waits for no one.' [AFB – 203, 204].

The problem of water mentioned by Mistry in his first novel, is again stated to be a problem in his second, emphasizing the gravity of the situation in Bombay. Dilnavaz in *Such a Long Journey* has a hectic time in the morning, filling up buckets and drums. The situation in the slum is worse, with children having to go without a proper bath for days together, being content with just wiping the body. Dina Dalal too, voices this concern with water.

> 'You can bathe and have tea here. As long as you wake up early, before the water goes. Keep in mind, I have only one bathroom.' [AFB - 474].

Along with the problem of water, another acute problem faced by Bombayites is the one of accommodation. It's such a serious problem that people turn downright hostile, not willing to entertain even friends and acquaintances. This is the reason why Nawaz behaved in the abominable way he did, with Ishvar and Om – once they overheard a conversation between Nawaz and his wife:

> 'The thing is, if I wanted people living under my back awning, I would rent it for good money. You know how dangerous it is, keeping them for so long ? All they have to do is file a claim for the space, and we'd be stuck in court for –" [AFB - 192].

It is for identical reasons like this that Dina Dalal does not readily agree to let the tailors sleep in the verandah, fearing they might lay a claim to the premises in due course. This leads to them being picked off the roads, along with the pavement dwellers. After being 'rescued' by Beggarmaster, Dina lets them sleep on her verandah, but refuses to accept money for it would mean sub-letting on her tenancy, which in turn might be strongly objected to by the present land-lord.

After the death of Rustom, Dina had gone back to her brother's house. Within three months, however, the landlord had issued a notice asking her to vacate the premises as it was no longer needed. But Nusswan advices her against it saying,

> 'But don't give up your right. Mark my words; thetime is not far – off when accommodation will be impossible to find in the city. An old flat like yours will be a gold mine.'
>
> 'It's true,' said Ruby. 'I heard that Putli Maasi's son had to pay a pugree of twenty thousand rupees just to get his foot in the door. And the rent is five hundred a month. His flat is even smaller than yours.' [AFB - 60].

The reader is a witness to the number of times Dina is troubled by the rent collector Ibrahim, when the landlord gets the wind of het using the flat for professional tailoring purposes. Many threats, notices, and attempts to frighten by sending goondas later, she is ultimately thrown out of her flat by the landlord by having bribed the policeman.

In between extremely difficult times, squalor and darkness in the lives of these four characters, there are some bright rays thrown in. Mistry uses this opportunity to remember the beautiful aspects of the city of Bombay – places of tourist interest where he sends Maneck and Om as a reward for having worked hard and behaving well in general. Dina tells Maneck.

> "All this time it's been home to class and class to home. But there is so much sightseeing in this city. The museum and aquarium and the sculpted caves will fascinate you. Victoria Garden and the Hanging Gardens are also worth visiting, believe me." [AFB - 506].

Over the next few pages the lively sights and sounds of Bombay come alive on the pages of the novel as described by Om and Maneck for the benefit of Dina and Ishvar. The reader can visualize the rough sea with the 'launch jumping like a wild horse' on it, the beautiful fish with their 'stylish' swimming, the masseurs at the beach with their collection of 'Oils and lotions and towels'. Mistry takes a walk down memory lane with his fond remembrance of the museum:

> For three evenings he and Dina heard all about the Chinese gallery, Tibetan gallery, Nepalese gallery, samovars, tea urns, ivory carvings, jade snuff boxes, tapestries.
>
> Particularly transfixing had been the Armour collection – the suits of mail, jade-handled daggers, scimitars, swords with serrated edges ... bows and arrows, cudgels, pikes, lances, and spiked maces. [AFB - 508].

As in the first novel, the 'clanging milkmen' and 'argumentative crows' – important part of a typical town, find their rightful place in the pages. Mistry also cannot refrain from mentioning the monsoon in Bombay.

> Rain was pounding the street. Someone's motorcycle lay covered under a loudly thrumming tarpaulin. The puddles around it were muddy and uninviting. There were no children playing or splashing, the street joy – less in this rain that had stayed too long and was too torrential. [AFB - 509].

For Dina, the rain has romantic overtones. Her courtship with Rustom had continued through the monsoon, with him offering her his raincoat to keep dry and bringing a beautiful green coloured umbrella in the shape of a pagoda when he had first visited her house. She suggests that the boys need not be at home due to the rains.

> 'You think the whole city pulls a blanket over its head because of a little rain? Take the umbrella, it's hanging from the cupboard in your room.' [AFB – 511].

The happy reminiscences apart, Bombay, in *A Fine Balance* has been described as a 'story factory' by Om:

"It's not us, it's this city, 'said Om. 'A story factory, that's what it is, a spinning mill.' [AFB - 470].

From the widely peopled space and chaotic canvas of *A Fine Balance,* Mistry's *Family Matters* (2002), seems to have sunk considerably in the expanse covered. But it is the territory of the workings human of the mind that is at stake here, delving into areas of human psychology. Nilufer Bharucha opines :

It is a book which is very 'big' in compassion – it is indeed Mistry's most compassionate book to date. At the age of 50, from his Canadian point of vantage, Mistry has viewed the life of a middle – class Parsi family in Bombay in the mid – 1990s.[15]

Mistry's third novel, *Family Matters*, short listed for the Booker Prize and winner of the seventh annual Kiriyama Prize for literature of the Pacific Rim and the South Asian sub continent, is a saga of the Vakeel and Chinoy families and the times they live in. At the helm of affairs is Nariman Vakeel, a 79 year old Parsi widower. In his old age Nariman is beset with Parkinson's disease, hypertension and osteoporosis. Once a witty and genial former teacher of English literature to college students, Nariman refuses to be bothered and bossed over by his step children, Coomy and Jal.

Mr. Kapur, the erstwhile proprietor of Bombay Sporting, a shop selling goods required for sports says,

"Let us sit upon these chairs, and tell sad stories of the death of cities." [FM]

Sarah Curtis' comments in her review of *Family Matters* quite pertinent on this subject:

Tumultuous Bombay, in its new incarnation as Mumbai, is at the centre of Rohinton Mistry's story, as it was in his previous two novels which were both short-listed for the Booker Prize. Ever since *Tales from Firozsha Baag*, his collection of short stories published in 1987, he has been unraveling threads, my theologizing and teaching lessons from the city of his birth.[16]

With all the shortcomings of old age, compounded by diseases as noted above, Nariman, nevertheless is reluctant to miss his daily walks. His step-children, both middle aged now, discourage this urge of his, as much for his safety, as much for any inconvenience it would bring them.

> "Even with my healthy legs, pappa, walking is a hazard, "said Jal, continuing the daily fun over his stepfather's outing. "and lawlessness is the one certainty in the streets of Bombay. easier to find a gold nugget on the footpath than a tola of courtesy. How can you take any pleasure in a walk?" [FM - 3].

Through Jal's misgivings, Mistry voices his concern on two aspects of Bombay, one already deliberated upon in his first two novels, 'goonda raj' and 'government atrocities' in *Such a Long Journey;* and protectors of the Law working hand-in-gloves with those that break it, Sergeant Kesar along with the landlord's goondas evicting Dina from her flat, and again Sergeant Kesar 'selling' beggars from the streets to the facilitator to work in labour camps in *A Fine Balance.* In the present novel, it has references to the renewed animosity between Hindus and Muslims post Babri Masjid episode. References are made to an incident, when

> "The goondas who assumed Muslims were hiding in Dalal Estate and set fire to it ?" [FM - 4].

> "Just last week in Firozsha Baag an old lady was beaten and robbed," said Jal. "Inside her own flat. Poor thing is barely clinging to life at Parsi General." [FM -5].

The hazards of walking mentioned by Jal in the quotation from page 3 of the novel refers to the numerous ditches, potholes and unruly traffic, not to say of the pavements being taken up by various vendors of vegetables, flowers, fruits and bhel-puri.

> The bhel-puri stall was a sculptured lands cape with its golden pyramid of sev, the little snow mountains of mumra, hillocks of Puris, and, in among their valleys, in aluminum containers, pools of green and brown and red chutneys. [FM –6].

Coomy and Jal's fears, regarding possible dangers that might befall their stepfather turn into a reality with him returning home with a slight limp and abrasions on his elbow and forearm. He explained that he had tripped on something and twisted his ankle while crossing the lane outside Chateau Felicity. The gift that Roxana and Yezad get for Nariman's birthday, a walking stick made of walnut has Coomy gaping in disbelief and Jal reiterating his earlier statements on why one should not take a walk on the streets of Bombay.

> "The streets are a death trap, "began Jal. Footpaths are dry up, pedestrians have to compete with traffic, dozens of fatalities daily. We told Pappa to stroll around the flat for exercise, it's big enough. For fresh air he can use the balcony. Why risk life and limb on those murderous pavements ?"
>
> "I think you are overreacting," said Yezad. "I agree you have to walk cautiously, not rely on traffic signals. But it's still a civilized city." [FM – 3.5].

Yezad's supplications make the reader think that Bombay, with all its shortcomings still holds its joys for the staunch Bombayite.

In his third novel too, Mistry creates space for the Bombay monsoon. The Chenoy family arrive for Nariman's birthday in a heavy downpour.

> Jal let the family in and ran with their umbrellas and raincoats to the bathroom to prevent a puddle by the door. He returned with a cloth, mopping the trail of water. After everyone finished wiping their rain-shoes on the mat, he led them to the drawing-room. "That's a big shower you got caught in." [FM - 19].

On their way back, Mistry describes the effects of the rain on the streets of Bombay, carefully recording every remembered detail.

> They were the only ones at the bus stop, where a large puddle had collected on the broken pavement. The wet road was glossy black in the street light, shimmering and hissing under the wheels of passing traffic. [FM –42].

At the bus stop, two men in a drunken state leer at Roxana, prompting Yezad to correct his earlier statement issued in defense of Bombay. "Some things can't be ignored. Maybe Jal is right; Bombay is an uncivilized jungle now." [FM - 45].

The drunkards' singning "Choli Kay Peechhay Kya Hai" with an exaggerated leer towards Roxana visibly frightened her and the children and angered Yezad. It must be noted at this point that the singing of this film song is the only reference to the flourishing film industry of Bombay which surprisingly does not find mention in the fictional work of Mistry. This is surprising for the reader since all other aspects of Bombay, namely its landmarks, places of tourist interest, local trains, BEST buses, the monsoon, even the ubiquitous crow and milkman find repeated references. The only reason that could be attributed to this finding is that maybe Mistry was not sufficiently influenced by the film industry to make him want to record it in his fiction.

Once on the bus, Roxana fondly remembers the Hanging Gardens, where they used to stroll around when still unmarried. The bus route mentioned is the Sandhurst Bridge turn to Hughes Road. Nariman's penchant for taking evening walks lands him in real trouble. With the rains having let up after pouring relentlessly for the last fifteen days, Nariman had dared to venture out, and fallen in a ditch dug up by the telephone company. The fall lands him up in bed with a broken ankle, encased in a plaster of Parsis cast right down from his thigh to the ankle. The pleasures of walking on the 'dangerous' roads of Bombay, thus cost him dearly. Mistry does not lose the opportunity to mention the numerous processions which hold up the traffic in Bombay.

Soon after emerging from the hospital gates, they came to a standstill near the main intersection where a political procession was making its way.

> "What party is it ?" asked Nariman. "Who knows. It's hard to read the banners from here. BJP, JD, CP, VHP, BSP, doesn't matter, they're all the same ... They waited for the traffic to start moving again. [FM – 60].

The un-informed reader, after having read all three novels of Mistry would definitely understand how acute the shortage of water in Bombay is. The problem as presented by Mistry in the first two novels, has already been noted. In the present one, *Family Matters,* the problem is first mentioned by Coomy, when Nariman needs toilet paper to be cleansed,

> "But I have some, "said Coomy". " I bought a few rolls last year during the water shortage. Luckily, we never had to use them." [FM - 72].

In Roxana's house, the crisis is worse, with the boys being allowed a bath only on alternate days, with Yezad having the privilege of a daily bath.

Jehangir wondered whether he would ever feel about bathing as Murad did. Daddy was the only one with the privilege of bathing every day because he had to go to work and meet customers. [FM - 92].

> "It's your turn today, and that's final," said his mother. "If Murad wants a daily bath he must get out of bed before the tap goes dry. At six, like me." [FM – 93].

When Nariman is unceremoniously dumped in a plaster cast by Coomy and Jal, Roxana has no alternative but to make the most of resources to look after her ailing father. She proceeds to put on fresh clothes for him, removing the dirty smelly ones, and laments the shortage of water.

She apologized that there was not enough water for a full sponge bath, and promised to save a bucket for tomorrow.

> "I told you this morning, don't force me to take a bath, "said Jehangir. ... Roxana crumpled the sudra to wipe the sweat from her father's back and armpits. She shook powder from the tin and rubbed briskly, again lamenting the lack of water. [FM - 111].

With Nariman having retired as a professor of English several years back and spending most of his savings on buying a flat for Roxana and Yezad on their wedding, Coomy finds it very difficult to run the house on Nariman's meager pension. It is at this juncture that the all important share bazaar of Bombay is introduced by Mistry.

> "Jal will tell you how hopeless the share bazaar is, Mamma's investments make barely enough to let us eat dal-chaaval. And you know better than anyone, Pappa used up all his money to pay for your flat." [FM - 35].

> Jal missed another morning at the share bazaar. [FM - 78].

> "We ? You run off every morning to the share bazaar." [FM –172].

All these instances from the text prove how important the share bazaar is in Jal's life, and many others like him. They also drive home the point that looking after investments in the share bazaar in order to yield a regular income, needs as much time and devotion as would a full-time job.

Along with the share bazaar, another similar institution, of the Matka, finds equal coverage in the text. Mattka, though illegal, is however very popular and has permeated the very fabric of Bombay. It is this unauthorized game of gambling that Yezad takes refuge in when he needs to supplement his income to meet the growing cost of his father-in-law's medicines. He, at one time, used to make fun of Villie Cardmaster, the spinster who stays with her mother in the same building as theirs. Villie is nicknamed 'Matka Queen' by Yezad and it is she who guides him in his investments in Matka. He begins by winning small amounts, which encourage him to gradually bet larger amounts.

Gautam said for most people Matka was a harmless bit of fun, like buying a lottery ticket. "Basically, however, it's a criminal scourge that has Bombay helpless in its grip." [FM - 206].

> "... But Matka also finances Shiv Sena machinery. And Matka money paid for the plastic explosives with which the terrorists blew up the stock exchange. You see the paradox ? The enemies of the nation, and political parties that claim to be defenders of the nation, all rely on the same source." "Problem is, "said Vilas, "So do millions of ordinary people.

> The numbers they bet each night give them reason to wake up next morning. In some ways Matka is Bombay and Bombay is Matka." [FM - 207].

> As luck would have it, Yezad on a winning spree, and somewhat reckless with his winnings, empties Roxana's envelopes, with her careful budget for the month, and bets it all, expecting an astronomically high figure to take care of all his troubles, loses it all together when police shut down Matka one night. She said the police were arresting people from top to bottom – big bookies and small, kingpins and little safety pins. Rumour was that since those terrorist bombs had blown up the stock exchange and shattered Bombay, they had to do something about Matka. Even the crookedest politician didn't want Bombay to be the next Beirut. [FM - 271].

Here Mistry comes under a scathing attack from critic Nilufer E. Bharucha, who opines that for a person who had lived in Bombay when the said bomb blasts rocked the city, Mistry's cursory reference to the incident is quite disturbing.

> Also, a little disturbing for someone who has lived through the tumultuous period from 12 December 1992 to 12 March 1993, is that there is only a passing reference to the series of bomb blasts that rocked Bombay on the latter date. Mistry's political consciousness and acumen thus begs comparison with another diasporic book on that same troubled and shameful time that Bombay went through – Salman Rushdie's *The Moor's Last Sigh.* Rushdie's in-the-face tackling of the complicity of the Shiv Sena in the Hindu-Muslim riots that rocked Bombay in the wake of the demolition of the Babri Masjid, in Ayodhya in Northern India, by militant Hindu mobs, while the state administration stood by as mute witnesses, is papered over in Mistry's book.[17]

The discerning reader, making a close study of Mistry's novels, would be able to identify his Bombay 'faithfuls'. One of them is the local train. Yet what is worth noticing is the fact that different aspects of the local trains are discussed in each text. If a train route is meticulously traced out in *Such a Long Journey, A Fine Balance* describes the general bonhomie present within local trains, as also the tracks being a favourite site for committing suicides. *Family Matters* treats yet another aspect, that of referring to trains by the time they arrive on a particular station, and not their names.

> The nine – eleven left the station as Yezad arrived at the platform. He fought his way into the nine- seventeen; the train moved out with men running alongside.
>
> Grabbing an overhead railing, he chose to stay near the exit – too far in would mean a return struggle at Marine Lives. He squeezed himself nearer one of the fans, though, to minimize his own sweating and the smell of armpits around him.
>
> These tactical maneuvers were performed by instinct, the instinct for survival in the urban jungle, he used to joke with college friends– instead of tree branches, you swung from railings inside trains and buses, hung from bars outside them. [FM - 137].

Yazad's thoughts of 'the instinct for survival in the urban jungle' has echoes of 'survival of the fittest', which is the also the philosophy of life propounded by Mistry. Among the squalor and depravity present in Mistry's world, characters who have the will and the inclination to live on, do so, after making whatever adjustments were necessary. Another observation that needs to be made here is Yezad's description of a crowded train which has just started, 'with men running alongside'. A similar scene is further described by Mr. Kapur :

> "... A train was leaving, completely packed, and the men running alongside gave up. All except one. I kept my eyes on him, because the platform was coming to an end.
>
> Suddenly, he raised his arms. And people on the train reached out and grabbed them. What were they doing, he would be dragged and killed, I thought! A moment later, they had lifted him off the platform. Now his feet were dangling outside the compartment and I almost screamed to stop the train. His feet pedaled the air. They found a tiny spot on the edge, stepped off, found if again. [FM – 159, 60].

And so the incident was described by Mr. Kapur, who marveled at the total trust the man placed in the hands of total strangers, unmindful of their caste, creed or religion. In its pure simplicity, it amounted to ordinary human beings spontaneously reaching out to help another like themselves, without any thoughts of discrimination. Through this incident Mr. Kapur (Mistry) points to other larger, more poignant issues – the issues of the all encompassing, tolerant attitude of Bombay

> "You see, Yezad, Bombay endures because it gives and it receives. Within this warp and weft is woven the special texture of its social fabric, the spirit of tolerance, acceptance, generosity. Any where else in the world, in those so-called civilized places like England and America, such terrible conditions would lead to revolution." [FM - 159].

Sad with the state of affairs in Bombay, Mr. Kapur believes he should contribute his share in wiping out the evils that have befallen Bombay. He proposes to context the next municipal elections. To Yezad's questions as to the cause of this sudden desire, he answers:

> " I just told you – because Bombay is everything to me. No use complaining about crooks destroying it if –" [FM - 157].

Sharing bottles of beer after shop is closed for the day, their conversation continues:

> "You see how we two are sitting here, sharing ? That's how people have lived in Bombay. That's why Bombay has survived floods, disease, plague, water shortage, bursting drains and sewers, all the population pressures. In her heart there is room for everyone wants to make a home here." [FM – 158, 59].

This is Mistry's thinking also, that in spite of all these shortcomings, hundreds and thousands of outsiders flock to Bombay to also try and make it big in the city of opportunities. Mr. Kapur's (Mistry's) adulation of Bombay verges on the poetical:

> "This beautiful city of seven islands, this jewel by the Arabian sea, this reclaimed land, this ocean gift transformed into ground beneath our feet, this enigma of cosmopolitanism where races and religions live side by side and cheek by jow in peace and harmony, this diamond of diversity, this generous Godless who embraces the poor and the hungry and the huddled masses, this Urbs Prims in India, this dear, dear city languishes ..." [FM - 160].

Nilufer Bharucha, citing these passages from *Family Matters,* in her critical work on Mistry is of the opinion that Mistry is here quietly having fun at Salman Rushdie's expense.

> Could it be that Mistry is here tongue-in-cheek poking fun at Salman Rushdie's eulogizing of the fabled tolerance of the city in his *The Moor's Last Sigh,* through Mr. Kapur's almost poetic praise of the city ? ... The sly insertion of 'the ground beneath our feet' only lends further substance to the suspicion that Mistry is needling Rushdie here.[18]

Another point on which Mistry is critiqued by Bharucha is on his placing Irani tea shops and Shiv Sena in the same time frame.

> On the way to the Irani restaurant for their afternoon tea break, Vilas pointed to Mr. Kapur's Diwali display... In the restaurant he and Yezad skirted a mess of spills and over turned chairs by the entrance. Behind the counter stood Merwan Irani, huge and rotund at the open till... Just then, Vilas's friends appeared at the entrance. He moved them over and raised four fingers for the waiter as he introduced Gautam and Bhaskar to Yezad ... "I bet you," said Vilas, "Whichever Shakha those Shiv Sainiks came from, the police chowki in their neighbourhood knows exactly who they are," [FM – 204, 05, 06, 07].

Bhaskar and Vilas, who are journalists, have Khadi satchels slung over their shoulders and their jeans and satchels are patched at numerous places. Their conversation over tea and snacks span several burning topics including the growing menace of Shiv Sena. This is where Bharucha raises her finger pointing to the impossibility of such a situation. She argues that Irani tea shops in Bombay were just like the *addas* in Calcutta, where matters ranging from sports to politics and films were hotly debated and discussed by students, artists and intellectuals over cups of tea.

> Such cafes have today and even in the 1990s become a fondly remembered memory, as they have been taken over by international coffee shop chains or become fast-food outlets. Here Mistry's diasporic time warp is in evidence when he places Chinoy's conversations on the Shiv Sena's continuing degradations, among other topics, in an Irani tea-shop.[19.]

Mr. Kapur's conversations with Yezad often date back to the years of partition, 1947, when his family fled from present – day Pakistan and sought refuge in Bombay.

> "... But Bombay treated us well. My father started over, with Zero, and became prosperous. Only city in the world where this is possible." [FM - 151].

He further argues that his love for Bombay was much more intense than what people born and brought up in that city have for her. He professes unending love for, ready even to die for her cause.

> "... What I feel for Bombay you will never know. It's like the pure love for a beautiful woman, gratitude for her existence, and devotion to her living presence. If Bombay were a creature of flesh and blood, with my blood type, Rh negative – and very often I think she is – then I would give her a transfusion down to my last drop, to save her life." [FM - 152].

The last statement of Mr. Kapur proves to be strangely prophetic – he is murdered by a couple of Shiv Sainiks in his own shop, for having abused two of their colleagues who had demanded that he change the name of his shop from Bombay to Mumbai. Mr. Kapur had offered to pay money to retain Bombay, but they had been unrelenting, resulting in Mr. Kapur's pushing them out of his shop, with a lot of abuses. This murder of Mr. Kapur after his proclamation of not hesitating to die for

Bombay if the need arose, is strangely reminiscent of the late Prime Minister, Mrs. Indira Gandhi's assassination. She had proclaimed dramatically at a public meeting in Orissa, how she would not hesitate to give every drop of her blood for the cause of the nation if the need arose. Strangely enough, she was assassinated by her own body guards, at her own residence, within some days of this proclamation.

Once, Mr. Kapur procures pictures of Bombay taken almost six decades ago, from a private collector. He and Yezad have a wonderful time trying to recognize the present day Bombay in the old photographs. Mr. Kapur describes them as if they are of a baby's.

> "These are my beautiful Bombay's baby pictures. Priceless. Her time of innocence. Now look at the other one." [FM - 153].

The reader wonders whether it is Mr. Kapur who is in awe of the pictures or Mistry indulging in fond memories of a city constantly changing and evolving. As the novel progresses, we have visions of a mature Mr. Kapur (Mistry) redefining his vision of the present day Bombay, equating it to the all – embracing principles of Hinduism.

> "Remember I said Bombay is like a religion ? Well, it's like Hinduism. I think." ...
>
> "Hinduism has an all-accepting nature, agreed ? I'm not talking about the fundamentalists, mosque –destroying fanatics, but the real Hinduism that has nurtured this country for thousands of years, welcoming all creeds and beliefs and dogmas and theologies, making them feel at home ...".
>
> "The same way, Bombay makes rooms for everybody. Migrants, businessmen, perverts, politicians, holy men, gamblers, beggars, wherever they come from, whatever caste or class, the city welcomes them and turns them into Bombayites. So who am I to say these people belong here and those don't secular good, communal bad, BJP unacceptable, Congress lesser of evils?" [FM - 362].

The above quotation describes and accounts for the various types of characters who have filled the pages in his 'created' (Bharucha's term) version of Bombay. He has fashioned Bombay from newspaper reports, visits to the city and meeting friends and relatives from Bombay. Through the character of Yezad, Mistry seems to sympathise with people who badly wanted to migrate to western countries, but for various reasons were not successful. Almost in a consoling voice, he says.

> And he assuaged his disappointment by keeping track of problems in the land of excess and superfluity, as he now called it : unemployment, violent crime, homelessness, language laws of Quebec. Not much difference between there and here, he would think : we have beggars in Bombay, they have people freezing to death on Toronto streets; instead of high – and low-caste fighting, racism and police shootings; separatists in Kashmir, separatists in Quebec – why migrate from the frying pan into the fire ? [FM - 137].

This is Mistry's biting criticism of the halo around immigrating to Canada. He seems to be bursting the myth that people should not be fooled into believing that the grass is greener on the other side. Problems, opportunities exist on both sides equally. But in his case, his blossoming as a writer was possible only because he left his beloved Bombay behind.

> "The separation from Bombay helped make me a writer. It became achallenge to recreate the city, to write down Bombay."[20]

Rohinton Mistry's novels seem to resemble those of Thomas Hardy in more ways than one. They are all set in Bombay like Hardy's works in Wessex. Another striking feature common to both writers is the importance attributed to destiny/ chance in their fictional work.

In his view of life, Rohinton Mistry seems to resemble that of Hardy. At first sight, their novels present a gloomy view of life. Their faith in determinism makes him a pessimist, who sees no glory in life, little scope for happiness and perfection, man struggling in vain against an unsympathetic nature and adverse circumstances. Their characters seem to snatch at happiness, striving to express and fulfill themselves, but only breaking themselves against a power that takes no heed of them. The historical contemplation of Wessex in the case of Hardy and Bombay in the case of Mistry seem to be partly responsible for this gloomy view. The insignificance of man and the briefness of his life are always present in Hardy's mind.

The lives of Gustad Noble, Dina Dalal, Maneck Kohlah, Dukhi Mochi, Ishvar and Omprakash Darji, Mr. Kapur, Nariman, Yezad, Coomy and Roxana all bear testimony to this fact. They are helpless against the circumstances of life. They, at times, feel powerless against fate. Gustad cannot control Sohrab's not joining IIT, cannot help Roshan to get well quickly even though he would like to. Dina Dalal tries her best to remain independent, but has no control over prevailing circumstances. Her father dies, her mother dies, her husband dies, she still tries to hold her head high. Ultimately , when her eyesight fails, the tailors don't come back, she is forced to again seek shelter in her brother's house. Nariman wanted to marry Lucy, but married Yasmin instead, thus ruining three lives along with the lives of his step children, Coomy and Jal. Yezad, who does not believe much in religious practices becomes a bigot towards the end of the novel.

It should be noted that Hardy's philosophy of life is marked with a strong sense of fatalism. In Hardy's novels Destiny is character. Man is a helpless creature, a mere puppet at the hands of Destiny or Fate. Man in Hardy's world does not enjoy Free Will. The keen eyes of fate are always looking intently on his activities with a view to intervene as and when it so likes. Man is not free to choose the type of life he wants to live. Obstacles thwart his hopes and aspirations though he continues to wage a futile battle against the odds so created.

REFERENCES

1. Nilanjana S. Roy, 'Such a Long Book'. Rev. of *Family Matters. Biblio: A Review of Books.* Vol. 7, No. 5-6, May-June 2002. pp. 5-6.
2. Nilufer E. Bharucha, *Rohinton Mistry: Ethnic Enclosures and Transcultural Spaces,* Jaipur: Rawat Publications, 2003. p. 130.
3. *Ibid.*, p. 130.
4. *Ibid.*, p. 131.
5. *Ibid.*, p. 135.
6. *Ibid.*, p. 139.
7. David Williams, 'What's in a Name ? Changing Boundaries of Identity in *Such a Long Journey* and *The Puppeteer'*, *Postmodernism and Feminism* (Canadian Contexts), Ed. Shirin Kudchedkar, Pencraft India: New Delhi, 1995 p. 217.
8. Nilufer E. Bharucha, *Rohinton Mistry : Ethnic Enclosures and Transcultural Spaces,* Jaipur: Rawat Publications, 2003. p. 119.
9. Sudha P. Pandya, 'Narrating the Nation: Rewriting History in Meena Alexander's *Nampally Road* and Rohinton Mistry's *A Fine Balance',* in Nory Kapdia, *Parsi Fiction,* Vol. 2, New Delhi: Prestige Books, 2001.
10. Cyrus Mistry, *Sunday*, October 27, 1991.
11. Geoff Hancock, 'Interview with Rohinton Mistry', *The Canadian Fiction Magazine,* No. 65, 1989.
12. Savita Goel, 'A Literary Voyage to India : Rohinton Mistry's *A Fine Balance',* in Jasbir Jain, *Writers of Indian Diaspore : Theory and Practice,* Jaipur: Rawat Publications, 1998, p. 193.
13. *Ibid.*, pp. 193-194.
14. Nilufer E. Bharucha, pp. 154-155.
15. *Ibid.*, p. 169.
16. Sarah Curtis, 'Beyond Mumbai'. Rev. of *Family Matters. The Times Literary Supplement.* No. 5168, April 19-2002. p. 21.
17. Nilufer E. Bharucha, pp. 168-169.
18. *Ibid.*, p. 186.
19. *Ibid.*, p. 208.
20. Interview with John Bemrose.

4

Matters of the Family

This chapter critically examines the novels of Mistry with respect to various factors that constitute a family - Matters of the Family. In *Such a Long Journey* Mistry through the Family of Gustad Noble depicts the fine threads that constitute a Family. For Gustad, there is an extended sense of family which exists in Khodadad Building. Family for him also means relations with close friends like Major Jimmy Bilimoria, Dinshawji and the lame man, Tehmul Lungraa. Gustad at times is the only one who bothers about the well being of his friends more than their family does. In *A Fine Balance* Mistry creates a very different sort of family which consists of a Parsi widow, Dina Dalal, her paying guest, Maneck Kohlah and two tailors, Ishvar and Omprakash Darji Due to strange circumstances, these four people form an unlikely family, sharing each other's joys and sorrows. But as Maneck Kohlah says, 'everything ends badly'. The happy times shared by these people soon come to end. Maneck commits suicide, unable to face life anymore. In the novel Mistry also portrays the family of Monkey man, which consists of a pair of monkeys, named Laila and Majnoo and a dog, Tikka, besides himself. When the monkeys are killed by the dog, Monkey man kills the dog as a just retribution. In the third novel by Mistry, *Family Matters* , readers are brought face to face with a different family setup. Nariman Vakeel, a seventy nine year old, Parsi widower, stays with his two step-children, Coomy and Jal. He also has a daughter, Roxana, who lives with her husband and two sons in a small flat gifted to them by Nariman. Nariman after meeting with an accident is unceremoniously dumped in Roxana's tiny flat by Coomy and Jal. The readers are then treated to the delicate family relationships that already exist and further deepen between the grandfather and his two grandsons, Murad and Jehangir. Mistry seems to be making a very strong comment on the shabby way old people are treated by their families. Critics claim this book to be Mistry most mature one. Bharucha feels that Mistry should stick to writing about family relations more than political ones.

Mistry's fictional world has been compared in its microcosmic quality to R.K. Narayan's Malgudi novels. Despite all the references to the public world, religious intolerance and historical injustice, the author is less concerned with public events than with the lives of individuals and families, their personal tragedies and social lives. His strength lies in his capacity to invoke transparency, his dexterity at erasing the boundary between life and artifice. Mistry's novels concern family life within an Indian Parsi social frame. Individual stories, what Dan Coleman calls the 'romance' of family progress' has been a major concern in his fiction. N.S. Dharan opines:

> *Such a long Journey,* Mistry's first novel, is a moving domestic tragi – comedy that introduces readers to Gustad Noble, a devout Parsi and dedicated family man, who becomes enmeshed in the political turmoils of the Indira Gandhi years.[1]

Gustad Noble, a middle class Parsi man is the protagonist of *Such a Long Journey.* He lives with his family, which consists of his wife Dilnavaz, and his three children, Sohrab, Darius, and Roshan. They live in a Parsi housing enclave, Khodadad Building, which houses most of the other Parsi Characters portrayed in the text. According to Amritjit Singh,

> The world of the Khodadad Building in his new novel is but an extension of Firozsha Baag. Either of these two fictional locations forms a microcosm in itself – all its diverse cast of characters with their ordinary human struggles and their extraordinary range of eccentricities.[£]

In the beginning of the novel, Gustad is portrayed as an affectionate husband and doting father. He watches his sleeping children with fatherly pride:

> And so, as he watched Sohrab sleep his innocent sleep, with the face that seemed on the verge of a smile, shorter reflection of his father's muscular frame; and little Roshan, who filled such a small part of the bed – with – the – door, her two plaits sidelong on the pillow : as Gustad observed them silently, in turn, he wished for all the nights in his son's and daughter's lives to be filled with peace and tranquillity. [SaLJ - 9].

Gustad's own ambitions in youth were badly spoilt, which led to his entertaining hopes for his elder son, Sohrab to join the IIT. Through Sohrab's success, he has visions of the shattered dreams of his embittered youth ultimately bearing fruit. Unfortunately, however, Sohrab refuses to comply with his father's wishes and flatly says no to joining the IIT, saying his interests lay elsewhere. This leads Gustad to retaliate in anger, disbelief and frustration.

> 'What have we been all these years if not patient? Is this how it will end ? Sorrow, nothing but sorrow. Throwing away his future without reason. What have I not done for him, tell me ? I even threw myself in front of a car. Kicked him aside, saved his life, and got this to suffer all my life.' He slapped his hip. 'But that's what a father is for. And if he cannot show respect at least, I can kick him again. Out of my house, out of my life ?' [SaLJ - 52].

Gustad always strives to bring happiness for his family. To celebrate Roshan's ninth birthday and Sohrab's passing the entrance exam for IIT, he decides to get a chicken, live from Crawford Market, to be slaughtered at home and cooked, just like if was done in his family in childhood. Scenes from his childhood flash across his mind's eye, when there used to be many occasions for happiness and family get-togethers.

> There was much excitement and happiness filling his beloved childhood home, the sadness in his heart was acute when he awoke. He could not remember the exact occasion being celebrated in the dream – probably some birthday or anniversary. But live chickens had been brought home from the market by his father, and fattened for two days before the feast. And what a feast it had been. [SaLJ - 19].

A visit to the infamous Chor Bazar of Bombay, according to Major Bilimoria's directions, again takes Gustad down memory lane when he as a child had visited Chor Bazar with his father and bought a Meccano set. To the delight of everyone in the family he had fashioned many different models, and everyone predicted that he would make the family proud when he grew up. Those idyllic happy family memories are however blighted with remembrances of great misfortunes that later befall the happy Noble family. Gustad's father had been ailing for months together, but had put off the impending operation until the time had come for him to be rushed to hospital in an emergency. His father had stubbornly refused to heed to anybody's advice and handed over the charge of his prosperous bookstore to his good for nothing, drunkard brother. The inevitable followed, with Gustad's uncle squandering away the family fortunes, leaving the family in dire straits and the book shop declared bankrupt. Gustad's mother could not bear the strain of it, and had to be hospitalized. There she was in a state of shock, uncomprehending of the circumstances around her, and eventually, soon breathed her last. His 'once invincible' father broke down, cried bitterly and begged for Gustad's forgiveness for having failed him in not helping him to finish his college education. This show of weakness on his father's part hardened him considerably.

> He began to utter scornful things, while silently swearing to himself, then and there, that he would never divulge in tears – not before anyone, nor in private, no matter what suffering

> or sorrow fell upon his shoulders; tears were useless, the weakness of women, and of men who allowed themselves to be broken. [SaLJ-101].

The disappointment he faced as a teenager, and the circumstances which led to the disintegration of his family, instead of breaking his spirit, only burnished him further for the future. He strived to do everything that was in his power to make his family comfortable – the happiness and well being of his family mattered to him above everything else. When Roshan's chronic stomach ailment showed no signs of improvement, he did everything that was in his power and more to make things comfortable for her, hiding his own anxiety.

> Gustad went to the bed-with-the-door with the new mixture and pills. Dr. Paymaster had changed Roshan's prescriptions four times in the last fortnight, and ordered blood tests, stool tests, and barium X-rays. Last week, Gustad had sold his camera to pay the bills. [SaLJ - 170].

Roshan, a delicate and fragile little girl has her father lavishing tender affections upon her. When Sohrab and Darius were growing up, he tried to fulfil their desires of trying out new hobbies and experiment with new things, in spite of straitened circumstances.

> Most of his *sudras* had rents in them, and Dilnavaz kept fretting that a new batch was needed. Mending was useless – no sooner was one tear sewn up than another appeared because the mulmul itself was worn. He told her not to worry: 'A little air – conditioning does no harm,' laughing away, as usual, the signs of their straitened circumstances. [SaLJ-15].

Gustad was used to forgoing his basic requirements in order to be able to provide for his sons' growing interests. Sohrab developed an interest in catching butterflies and moths, killing them with the help of petrol, drying them up with the help of a drying agent, and finally mounting them in display cases. Darius' interests in keeping varieties of fish, all kinds of birds – finches, parrots, sparrows, lovebirds, etc., and a squirel, were all lovingly indulged in by the doting Gustad. For the sake of his son, he used to make the rounds of Crawford Market, which he otherwise despised, and got the animals demanded, expensive as they were. When Gustad and Dilnavaz are worried and at their wits end over Roshan's illness, Dilnavaz lashes out:

> 'Don't deny it ! From the beginning you have spoilt the boys ! Not for one single thing have you ever said no! Not enough money for food or school uniforms, and *baap* goes and buys airplanes, and fish tanks and bird cages!' [SaLJ – 166, 67].

The bitter exchange of words between husband and wife is overheard by Roshan who immediately wants to put a stop to it.

> 'I don't like if when you fight,' she said through her tears ... 'No, no, no. I cannot sleep till you kiss. Mummy will come here. 'When Dilnavaz did not move ... ' Not like that !' said Roshan, frustratedly pounding the arm of the chair. That's not a real Mummy – Daddy kiss. Do it like when Daddy goes to work in the morning. 'Dilnavaz rested her lips against Gustad's. 'Eyes closed, eyes closed!' yelled Roshan. 'Do it properly!' [SaLJ - 167].

The novelist gravely observes that Roshan having realized that a mere, cursory joining of the lips was not enough to do away with the anger and bitterness that grown-ups sometimes felt, quietly went to bed. The reported quarrel mentioned above and nine year old Roshan's doing her bit to put an early end to it speak volumes about the close knit family ties that hold a family together in times of adversity. Though Roshan's attempt to stop her parents from fighting might be a common occurrence in families, it is nevertheless quite touching to observe the power that children lovingly exude over their parents. It also serves to prove the point that many a times children become the reason of families not falling apart and disintegrating.

The love and affection showered by Gustad on his eldest child, Sohrab, is reciprocated by the latter in his genuine advice and concern meted out to his father whenever the need arises. When the macrocosm (Major Bilimoria enlisting Gustad's help in depositing ten lakhs) threatens to impinge on the microcosm (Gustad's family), it is but natural that members of the microcosm rally around the troubled one and offer all possible help. So it is the case with Sohrab, when he learns of the Major's letter, forgets the bitter show of displeasure on his father's part the night before and offers genuine advice.

> '... But what about the leaders who do wrong? Like the car manufacturing licence going to Indira's son ? He said Mummy, I want to make motorcars. And right away he got the licence. He has already made a fortune from it, without producing a single Maruti. Hidden in Swiss bank accounts. 'Dilnavaz listened intently as ... She was the self-appointed referee between father and son, her facial expressions registering the scores. [SaLJ - 69].

Gustad's affection for his wife is touchingly portrayed in the way he never forgets to put down a few words by way of note when the dubbawalla collected the lunch boxes to be taken back home. The pencilled note,

> ... was the one constant in their lives, always written and always read, no matter how much they fought or quarrelled. Until today. The daily notes did not say much : "My Dearest, Busy day today, meeting with manager. Will tell you later. Love & XXX' Or: 'My Dearest, *Dhandar – paatyo* was delicious. Aroma made everyone's month water. Love & XXX.' [SaLJ-70].

Later again, in the midst of their quarrel, he utters words, which though come out as an angry outburst, nevertheless are proof of his concern for his wife.

> '... You ungrateful woman ! why do you think I said not to boil ? For your sake ! as it is, you are so busy in the morning, running from bathroom to kitchen, with no time even to sit and drink your tea!' (SaLJ-166].

Such bonds make a family stronger. It is not only Gustad who sacrifices his comfort and toils hard for the sake of his family. In Dilnavaz too, the novelist has painted a caring mother, who puts service to her family over self in all matters. Her character would be dealt with in detail in the next chapter of the book.

Gustad's caring nature extends beyond his immediate family to other people in society – people from Khodadad Building, his colleagues at the bank, and sometimes people from the underprivileged section of society. For eg., once outside the Aarey Colony milk booth, he saw three boys and a girl in tattered clothes examining the used bottles for any trace of milk. The booth attendant warned them time and again not to do so. The children did not pay heed, which resulted in the attendant resorting to beating the girl. Gustad stopped him from doing so and decided to buy a bottle of milk for the girl, who appeared to him a skinnier version of Roshan. What took him by surprise was the girl stopped sipping the milk after the few initial ones, and held the bottle out to her three brothers. On Gustad's query, she answered:

> 'My brothers. They also like milk, 'she said shyly, looking down and tracing a design in the dust with her toe. [SaLJ-200].

The point Mistry wants to drive home through this brief but touching episode is that feelings of familial love exists even among the poor, down trodden and underprivileged class. The little beggar girl, deprived herself, yet is not selfish – the one spark of joy that comes to her life is not grabbed, but shared equally with her siblings.

Gustad's relationship with Major Jimmy Bilimoria also crosses the fine barrier between friend and brother. His children refer to Bilimoria as 'Major Uncle'.

> "But although Gustad would not admit it, Jimmy Bilimoria had been more than just a neighbour. At the very least, he had been like a loving brother. Almost one of the family, a second father to the children. Gustad had even considered appointing him as their guardian in his will, should something untimely happen to himself and Dilnavaz. [SaLJ - 14].

Major Bilimoria, along with Gustad, was in the habit of reciting the *Kusti* prayers every morning in the compound of Khodadad Building. When Gustad had been involved in an accident which broke his hip, it was the Major who carried him like a baby to Madhiwalla Boresetter for an alternative method of treatment – which had been a sensible decision. Every Sunday, the Noble family looked forward to the arrival of the Major for lunch, which consisted of special *Dhansaak* made by Dilnavaz. And the children loved to hear him narrate his various exploits.

> For his young listeners, the stories quickly acquired the stature of legend, with their Major Uncle the legendary hero, as he told of the cowardly Pakistanis who turned tail and ran in 1948, when confronted by Indian soldiers in Kashmir, or about the ... the crossing of Banihal Pass, the battle for Baramullah, the siege of Srinagar – were so fascinating that Gustad and Dilnavaz too would listen, enthralled. [SaLJ - 13].

Such was Major Bilimoria's relationship with the Noble family, that when he suddenly disappeared from Khodadad Building an year ago, without a word to anybody, it was much more than they could bear. As suddenly as he had disappeared, a letter arrived from nowhere, requesting Gustad's help for a secret mission. After much deliberation on the subject, he thought of helping the Major, which met with some resistance from his family:

> 'All this time, it has been Major this and Major that. I said forget him, he is vanished like a thief. But no. Now he writes for help, I say yes, and you are still not pleased.' [SaLJ]

Another person in the novel with whom Gustad has a very close relationship is his colleague at the bank, Dinshawji, also a fellow Parsi. In the absence of Major Bilimoria,' it is Dinshawji who is invited by Gustad to the birthday party of Roshan, which is further rendered special by the chicken dish which has been cooked after a gap of several years in the house. Dinshawji, very jovial by nature, has the ability to turn a conversation on the livelier side. When the atmosphere gets somewhat tense at the party, he tries his bit to ease the situation.

> Dinshawji, sensing the necessity, tried a diversion. 'Gustad, I think your Darius wants to make an *oollu* out of me. Says he can do fifty push-ups and fifty squats.' [SaLJ - 40, 41].

Very easily, he develops a camaraderie with Roshan and Darius, taking turns at singing songs and comparing biceps, composing poems on mundane, everyday topics and singing the birthday song.

> I wiss you health, I wiss you wealth,
> I wiss you gold in store;
> I wiss you heaven on earth,
> what can I wiss you more ? [SaLJ - 46].

In short, it is Dinshawji, the guest for the evening, an outsider, who tries wholeheartedly to sustain a joyful atmosphere in the family dinner, and without whom any semblance of happiness in the festivities would have been difficult to maintain. On another occasion, when Dinshawji comes for an important discussion with Gustad, he does not find the latter home. He finds Roshan, ill and weak, and spends some very enjoyable moments with her. The childless Dinshawji plays like a child with Roshan. They go through all the traditional, childhood games – *Arrung – Darrung*, *Kaakareya Kumar, Ekka-Per-Chaar,* etc.

From the way Dinshawji refers to his wife as the 'domestic vulture', it seems all is not hunky – dory between him and Alamai. The others in the bank have their lunches delivered fresh and hot by the dubbawallas. Dinshawji's wife, however, is in the habit of giving him a packed lunch in the morning, which generally consists of leftovers from the night before, put between two slices of bread.

> He often turned up with gems like cauliflower sandwiches, brinjal sandwiches, French bean sandwiches, pumpkin sandwiches, and ate them cheerfully, soggy bread and all. If he was teased about his epicurean delights, he would

say, 'whatever my dear domestic vulture gives, I eat without a word. Or she will eat me alive.' [SaLJ - 70].

This is the way Dinshawji maintains peace in his own family, strictly following the adage, 'what can't be cured has to be endured'. So he endured the various atrocities meted out to him by his wife. This pathetic condition is further highlighted when he lies critically ill in hospital, and his wife does not visit him for days together. It is Gustad who provides him with company at least twice a week, humouring him with news from the bank, etc. On one such occasion, Dinshawji's food is served in the hospital, and it is Gustad who helps him out by adjusting the level of bed and even feeding his friend.

> Dinshawji dipped the spoon in the bowl and conveyed it to his month. But his hand shook wildly, the soup dribbled throat wards down his chin. He smiled sheepishly, trying to wipe it with the back of his hand. Hesitantly, Gustad unfolded the napkin and cleaned him up. When Dinshawji let him do that without protest, he took the spoon and began feeding him. 'A little bread with it?' [SaLJ - 218].

Dinshawji is rendered tearful by this touching gesture of Gustad, and the reader is likewise impressed with the deep bonds of friendship, bordering on the familial which exists between the two 'colleagues'. Dinshawji was very popular in the bank as well and enjoyed a tremendous bonhomie with his colleagues.

The lunch hour in the canteen used to be spiced up with jokes on all the linguistic and ethnic groups; Sikhs, Madrasi, Guju, Pathan and even their very own Parsi. Sometimes song sessions replaced jokes, with everybody joining in.

> Lunch-time was the highlight of the drab working day. Invariably, Dinshawji was the star performer, the group hanging on to his every word. There were contributions from others too, but these seemed to pale in comparison. Dinshawji stored away everything he ever heard; weeks, even months later, he would bring it forth, refurbished and improved, a brand-new story. It was a necessary bit of plagiarism that no on minded. [SaLJ - 71].

His openly flirting with Laurie Coutino, the young typist and cracking jokes with sexual innuendoes earned him the little of 'the Casanova of Flora Fountain', which he enjoyed very much. This friendly, jovial nature of his saw him in good stead even on day of his death.

There was a large turnout at Doongerwadi. Few relatives, but many, many friends and colleagues. The news had taken them by surprise, so they were neither dressed in white nor had their prayer caps. But they managed somehow, the women draping their saris over the head, the men using handkerchiefs or borrowing caps from the sandalwood shop at the bottom of the hill. [SaLJ - 250].

Apart from these intimate friendships with Major Bilimoria and Dinshawji, Gustad has a healthy relationship with his neighbours at Khodadad Building, who are part of his extended family. Gustad has two bushes in his garden, a vinca and *subjo*. He has grown the vinca, while the *subjo* has appeared on its own. He is once ready to hack off the *Subjo*, but Miss Kutpitia happens to notice it and points out the medicinal properties of the plant. Soon neighbours begin to request Gustad for sprigs from the plant.

> Demand for Gustad's medicinal *Subjo* from Cavasji's household was constant, for Cavasji suffered from hypertension. Every day, his daughter-in-law fastened a fresh sprig of the mint on a string around his neck. As long as it dangled green and protective, his blood-pressure would not explode like his rage. [SaLJ – 87, 88].

Gustad is the only inhabitant of Khodadad Building who has any sympathy for the lame Tehmul Lungraa. Tehmul speaks incoherently and the neighbours consider it a waste of time to try and decipher the meaning of his utterances. It is only Gustad who indulges Tehmul, and treats him as a human being. On Tehmul's death, it is Gustad, who once again picks up the inert body and takes it to his flat, sits beside the body reciting appropriate passages from Ashem Vahoo and Yathu Ahu Varyo, shedding pent up tears just as is done on the death of a family member.

When it comes to lending a helping hand Gustad doesn't step back even when it is Miss Kutpitia, who is generally disliked for her interfering nature and strange, secretive ways. Yet Gustad is quick to respond to her call for help in shutting the windows which have been opened by the firemen to put out the fire. The windows had been opened after thirty five years and now could not be closed back.

> Gustad and Darius went readily to tackle the swollen windows, taking a chisel, sandpaper, two screwdrivers and the hammer. When they returned after an hour, Gustad remarked how Miss. Kutpitia had changed. 'Smiled at me, even made a joke, saying it was time I bought another rose for her. Earth-and-sky, difference in the old woman.' [SaLJ - 295].

Thus the tale of Gustad Noble is told, placed within the microcosm of Khodadad Building, which is related to the larger macrocosm of Bombay and politics at the National level, all of which have an influence on him and his family. Gustad finds himself powerless when pitted against the larger forces of destiny and politics, but there are happy moments, in which he takes pride and draws the strength to face the odds of life. Gustad's grand-father was a maker of fine furniture, and believed in making 'furniture as stout-hearted as his own being' [SaLJ - 254], so that 'when a piece of furniture was handed down, the family was enriched by much more than just wood and dowels.' [SaLJ - 254].

Ragini Ramachandra opines,

> Little wonder then if these relics of his childhood days stood like 'parentheses' around Gustad's entire life, indeed, the 'sentinels of his sanity'. Whenever therefore Gustad saw his son wielding his great grandfather's hammer, a sense of pride would well up within him.[3]

Gustad feels happy and cannot explain the complex emotions and words that arise within him.

> What did it mean when a hammer like this was passed from generation to generation? It meant something satisfying, fulfilling, at the deep centre of one's being. [SaLJ - 293].

The notion of the family, albeit in different forms can also be traced in *A Fine Balance,* Mistry's second novel. The novel has Mistry dealing with a cross-section of Indian society. This broadening of canvas is unlike what the author has done in his previous works of fiction. Yet the broad canvas necessarily encompasses a world which is similar to the ones evoked by Charles Dickens and George Eliot. Guy Lawson comments,

> 'Mistry and Dickens are interested in those to whom history happens, those with little control over their cirum-stances.[4]

So the reader is treated to detailed stories of the poor, downtrodden and underprivileged class, to vivid accounts of their trials and tribulations, obstacles, some of which are surmounted and some others which further bog them down. What connects through the diverse strands presented by Mistry is the willingness to share and help each other in spite of difficulties, the desire to reach out and comfort, creating a sense of fellow-feeling, a 'family', however temporary the bonds might be.

The first chapter of the novel begins with Dina Dalal nee' Shroff thinking in retrospect of the sheltered, perfect family life she enjoyed. In those days her father was a doctor, a GP, who was totally dedicated to his profession. His dedication takes him to remote villages with a team of other like minded people to serve hapless villagers, who otherwise have no access to medical aid. As luck would have it, Dr. Shroff dies from a cobra's bite, leaving behind his wife, daughter Dina, and son Nusswan to mourn the loss. After the initial, outward calm displayed by Mrs. Shroff, a gradual deterioration starts.

> It made little difference to Nusswan, who was twenty-three and busy planning his own future. But Dina, at twelve could have done with a parent for a few more years. She missed her father dreadfully. Her mother's withdrawal made it much worse. [AFB - 20].

The family, as it were, suddenly becomes rudderless, until Nusswan decides to take the reins in his own hands. He soon assumes the role of the head of the family and also the Royal guardian of Dina, sells off his father's dispensary, cuts down on hired help in the house and lays down various rules and regulations for Dina, making life miserable for her. She is told at what length her hair must be maintained, whether she can take part in school concerts or not, etc. Her life does not become easier with Nusswan's marriage to Ruby. Soon after their mother's death, Nusswan decides Dina should not continue with school, as her performance is not up to the mark. Dina rebels, but is not able to revert the situation. She tries to find happiness outside the house, as her family has reduced her to a household drudge. Her visits to free musical concerts bring her some solace and also help her meet Rustom Dalal, her future husband.

Dina's marriage to Rustom brings a lot of happiness into her life. She takes delight in looking after and organising the few items of furniture and utensils kept in the flat. She is contented with the meagre means at their disposal and does all that she can to make a 'home' of the 'house'.

> The dull blades soon began glinting with sharp edges. She relished the energy, the attention, the pounding and banging that went into getting her household shipshape for decades of wedded bliss with Rustom. A lifetime had to be crafted, just like anything else, she thought, it had to be moulded and beaten and burnished in order to get the most out of it. [AFB - 52].

Basking in the warmth of family life, they invite Dina's brother's family to dinner on their wedding anniversary. After Dina's marriage, relations between the two families had been cordial, erasing the bitter memories completely. On the fateful night of the wedding anniversary, Rustom dies in a ghastly accident and Dina, has no alternative but move in with her brother's family. For some time, Nusswan's positive shades of character take fore ground and they live quite amicably. Things begin to take a bad turn when Nusswan once again starts inviting eligible bachelors for Dina to choose from after the period of one year of mourning is over. Unable to stand his high-handed behavour, Dina decides in favour of shifting back to Rustom's flat. For solace and help she turns to Rustom's relatives, Shirin Aunty and Darab Uncle who give her the semblance of family. They welcome her with open arms.

> As always, Dina was touched by their happiness at seeing her. She felt their love pour over her like something palpable. It reminded her of the milk bath she was given as a child on her birthday, by her mother, when half a cup of warm milk, with rose petals afloat, came trickling down her face and neck and chest in tiny white runnels over her light-brown skin. [AFG – 65].

The much needed affection and empathy that Dina badly needs at this juncture of her life is provided not by her brother, (with whom she grew up as a child) and his family, but by the relatives of her dead husband, who make her feel a part of their family. Mistry seems to be discreetly saying here that sympathy and affection are rare unwarranted emotions and often come from unexpected quarters. By and by, these pillars on which she could lean on, become shaky, and finally crumble by their death and Dina is once again left alone wanting for family.

Dina's childhood friend, Zenobia, introduces her to Mrs. Gupta of Au Revoir, a company which undertakes export orders for clothes. The bulk piece order she undertakes, coupled with her failing eyesight necessitates hiring of two tailors for the smooth functioning of the job. Zenobia suggests Dina to also keep a paying guest to help with the expenses and thus the novelist introduces Maneck Kohlah, the son of a former school friend, Aban Sodawallah. A long, tedious search for the tailors proves to be fruitful and Ishvar and Omprakash Darji stage their entry.

Ishvar and Omprakash Darji, an uncle and nephew pair, hails from an unnamed 'Village by a river'. They belong to the *Chamaar* caste, with Ishvar's father being called *Dukhi Mochi*. Generations of meek submission to the higher castes of Brahmins and Thakurs, has the lower castes merely existing and not living out their lives. Dukhi Mochi dares to dream of a better life for his sons, Ishvar and Narayan, and puts them under the care of Ashraf, a Muslim tailor in the town. Ashraf and his wife Mumtaz, already have to look after their young daughters who gradually become four in number. Mumtaz at first resists their arrival in their cramped surroundings, until she hears Narayan's sobs of homesickness at night from the shop down below. At once, her motherly feelings are extended to the boys and Ashraf advices them to look upon his family as theirs.

Ashraf put his arm around him.

> 'When your father is not here, I stand in his place. And Mumtaz Chachi is like your mother, nah ? You can tell us anything you like. ... Ishvar nodded gravely. 'He thinks of home every night. I also think of if, but I don't cry.' ... 'But when it gets dark and everybody is sleeping, my father and mother come in my mind.' '... Ashraf held him on his lap, saying it was all right to think of his parents. ... He lay by their side till they fell asleep, and then crept upstairs with the lamp turned low. [AFG – 144].

Thus the boys like with Ashraf Chacha and Mumtaz Chachi looking upto them as parents, sharing their food, boarding and their happy and unhappy times. They live like a family and staunchly face all the misfortunes that befall them. Very soon riots between Hindus and Muslims break out and the place becomes rife with sordid tales of violence between the two communities, of trains arriving across the border full of corpses. And so the tales of violence continue, until Ashraf starts believing that the safest possible means of saving his family was to go away, across the border, into Pakistan. The neighbours rally around in his hour of need, reassuring him of all possible help and cooperation.

> 'Stay here. You are with friends. We will let nothing happen to your family. Where is there any trouble in our neighbourhood ? We have always lived here peacefully.'... 'Any time you went to, day or night, if you feel worried about anything, just come to our house with your wife and children.' [AFB – 154].

But the genuine, praiseworthy efforts to safeguard the interests of the shop and Ashraf's family are made by Ishvar and Narayan. They take down the board of Muzaffar Tailoring Company, and paint Krishna Tailors on the back side. When Ashraf Chacha takes down the Koranic quotations hanging on the wall, they quickly put up pictures of Ram and Sita, Krishna, and Laxmi in their place. The next night a group of twenty or thirty men collect outside the shop, demanding it to be opened. Ishvar and Narayan offer to go downstairs to tackle the problem, shielding Ashraf and his family. In the heated argument that follows, the group demands to be satisfied only when Ishvar and Narayan remove their pyjamas and allow themselves to be examined. They comply willingly; the crowd unanimously agreed that the foreskin was intact and quickly dispersed. The reaction of Mumtaz to the entire episode is one of deep gratitude.

> Mumtaz fell on her knees before the two apprentices. Her dupatta slid from around her neck and draped their feet. Please, Chachi, don't do that, 'said Ishvar, shuffling backwards.'
>
> 'Forever and ever, my life, my children, my husband's life, my home – everything, I owe to you!' She clung to them, weeping. 'There is no repayment possible!'...
>
> 'From now on, this home is your home, as long as you will honour us with your presence!' [AFB – 159 - 160].

Thus Mistry proves another point - affections within and outside the family, which is true of millions of such homes across India. With riots between Hindus and Muslims taking place throughout the country, two Hindu boys willingly and successfully protect a Muslim family from their Hindu oppressors. A situation with the religious group placed in opposite positions is also true and possible. Familial bonds reach across castes and religious, irrespective of ethnic groupings.

Times not being very propitious, only Narayan decides to go back to their family in the village and Ishvar stays on with Ashraf in the town. In due course Narayan marries Radha, but before that the bride viewing party that was arranged needs mention. Thirty eight people get into a vehicle which has the capacity of twenty seven. It is considered a prestigious issue to be part of the bride-viewing group.

> Roopa made certain that Amba, Pyari, Padma, and Savitri were included in plans for the visit – they were like family, she said ...
>
> 'Narayan is like a son to me,' said one. 'It's my duty to come. How can I let him down at this most important time?'
>
> 'I will not be able to hold my head up if you don't take me', pleaded another, refusing to take no for an answer. [AFB – 166].

Thus the merry party of villagers flock together as one family to attend a wedding. Mistry seems to be saying that the poor people of the village do not wait for an invitation card to reach them, or to be asked formally to be part of a celebration. The mere mention of it is enough for people to come together as one big, happy family. These poor people do not stay closeted inside their homes like the rich ones do, pretending ignorance at the goings-on around them. In due course Radha and Narayan have a son and two daughters. They live in a pukka house, which is one among seven in the village. The happy family now consists of the grandparents Dukhi and Roopa, the parents Narayan and Radha and their three children, Omprakash, Leela and Rekha.

The happiness, however, does not continue for a long time. At about the time Omprakash is fourteen years old, parliamentary elections are conducted. Around this time Narayan musters enough courage to want to cast his vote himself and not let the landlords men do as they want. His father Dukhi discourages these dangerous tendencies in his son. In the state assembly elections held two years later,

Narayan asserts his right to vote in the actual sense of the word. Two other voters in the queue with him echo his words. The men of Thakur Dharamsi, on his orders, seize the three 'voters', force their thumbprints on the appropriate places, hang them naked by their ankles from the branches of a banyan tree and flog them at regular intervals. After some more tortures, they are hanged to death and the bodies displayed in the village square. At about the same time, Thakur Dharamsi's goondas let loose a reign of terror in the untouchable section of the village, beating up and torturing individuals at random. But special punishment is reserved for Dukhi's family. The goondas are instructed to ensure that no one is spared. Roopa's friends, Amba, Pyari, Savitri and Padma try to raise an alarm, but are stopped by their respective families. All the family members of Dukhi except Ishvar and Om (who are away at the time) are bound up and dragged into the main room. Narayan's badly scarred and mutilated, barely recognizable body is brought in their presence.

> A long howl broke from Radha. But the sound of grief soon mingled with the family's death agony; the house was set alight. The first flames licked at the bound flesh. The dry winds, furiously fanning the fire, showed the only spark of mercy during this night. The blaze swiftly enfolded all six of them. [AFB – 180-181].

Mistry seems to make a very poignant comment here through this episode – entire families sometimes have to pay for the follies of single individuals, in this case, first Dukhi and then Narayan daring to rise against and change the existing order.

Not long after this ghastly incident, Ishvar and Omprakash who have been spared the fate their family suffered, because they were in town with Ashraf, have to seek their fortunes elsewhere, in the city by the Sea, as business in their small town dwindles.

Having tasted of Ashraf and his family's generosity, Ishvar and Omprakash arrive in Bombay, with Nawaz's address and high hopes of striking it big. Contrary to their expectations, however, Nawaz does not welcome them with open arms into his house or family. He does not offer them even a cup of tea, and only allows them to sleep outside the house, in the awning beside the kitchen. Nawaz abuses his wife for wanting to make tea for the tailors.

> Then from the front came his loud, surly tone again, 'No need for all that, I told you already.
>
> 'But it's just a little tea, 'said Miriam. ...
>
> 'Haramzadi! Don't argue with me! No means no! 'They heard the sharp sound of a slap, and Omprakash flinched. A cry escaped her lips. 'Let them go to a restaurant! The thing is, you pamper them and they'!! never leave!'
>
> ... 'But why ...' and then' ...
>
> Ashraf's family ...!
>
> 'Not my family, 'he spat. [AFB - 190].

Nawaz soon finds a shack in a slum for them to rent, and an offer to work for Dina Dalal as tailors. In an ironic tone the novelist describes how Nawaz invites them to have dinner with him in his house, the night before they leave, the first and only time in six months.

In the slum, however, they feel more at home, even with grave problems of water and toilet. For the first of these basic necessities they have to queue up along with others at the common tap and the second one takes them to the railway tracks. The only problem with this community toilet, however, is a functional knowledge of the railway timetable, failing which they might be surprised in the middle of the act by passing trains. They find a willing friend in Rajaram, who guides them through the new procedures and even offers them food from what he has cooked for himself.

> He poked the sizzling vegetables to check if they were done, then extinguished the stove and spooned out a helping on a plastic plate for the tailors.
>
> 'No, we ate at the station, really.'
>
> 'Don't insult me – have one bite at least.'
>
> They accepted the plate. [AFB - 208].

This incident is set in direct contrast to the recent shabby treatment meted out to them at Nawaz's. Mistry seems to be comparing the hospitality of the poor people with meagre means vis-à-vis the well to do. In the slum the inhabitants live like one extended family, sharing in each other's grief and happiness. One night they are awakened by piercing screams.

> People were emerging from shacks all down the row. Then word spread that it was a woman in labour, and everyone went back to sleep. The screams ceased after a while.
>
> In the morning, they heard that a girl had been born during the early hours. 'Let's go and give them good wishes.'said Ishvar. [AFB - 225].

Another interesting character they meet in the slums is Monkey–Man, so named for the two monkeys and a dog that are his means of livelihood. The three animals along with Monkey–Man live in a shack. The two monkeys are lovingly named Laila and Majnoo and the dog is called Tikka. The two monkeys ride the dog, performing tricks which fetch money for their owner. The monkeys torture the dog endlessly with their pinching and biting, but Tikka doesn't retaliate. The monkeys are also fed bananas by the Monkey–Man regularly while the dog is left to fend for himself in the garbage. Once all the inhabitants of the slum are forcibly taken to attend a public meeting of the then Prime Minister Indira Gandhi. Monkey–Man is left with no choice but lock up all three animals in the shack for the day. The sight that meets his eye on return is heart-rending Tikka has killed both the monkeys, and partially eaten one of them. Monkey–Man's first reaction is to kill the dog.

> 'I'll kill him!' Monkey–Man began wailing again. 'My babies are dead! I'll kill that shameless dog!' ... 'He played with them like brother and sister,' he wept. 'All three were like my children. And now this. I'll kill him.' ...
>
> They stayed with Monkey-man past midnight, letting him grieve for as long as he liked. A burial was planned for Laila and Majnoo, and they convinced him to forgive the dog. The

question of livelihood was raised by Rajaram. 'How long will it take you to train new monkeys?'

'They were my friends – my children! I don't want any talk of replacing them!'.

[AFB – 332-333].

Thus Monkey–Man grieves for his monkeys, buries them and even mourns them like one is expected to on the death of one's kin. In a world where people do not have time to grieve for their families (human beings), Monkey–Man bemoans the loss of his animals which are family to him.

The tailors go to work at Dina Dalal's house where they meet Maneck Kohlah, the paying guest. The readers are informed of Maneck's home in the mountains.

> Once, though, Maneck's family had been extremely wealthy. Fields of grain, orchards of apple and peach, a lucrative contract to supply provisions to cantonments along the frontier – all this was among the inheritance of Farokh Kohlah, and he tended it well, making it increase and multiply for the wife he was to marry and the son who would be born. [AFB - 248].

The novelist is quick to inform us that the vast fortunes of the Kohlah family fall a prey to the miseries of partition and the family assets were considerably reduced. Maneck's father, Farokh Kohlah, tried to get whatever was offered by way of compensation by the government. His mother, meanwhile managed the general stores single – handedly. Maneck, from a very tender age, enjoyed helping his parents in the shop. He had a wonderfully happy childhood in the idyllic mountains. He often remembers those moments of togetherness.

> At this hour, as the pan hissed and sputtered, the aroma of fried eggs would begin to travel upstairs and to the porch. The appetizing emissary would deliver wordless messages to Maneck and his father. Then Maneck would leave the moving – mist panorama and hurry to breakfast, hugging his parents, whispering good morning to each before sitting down at his place. [AFB – 243 - 244].

Maneck loved to breathe the pure mountain air like his father and his forefathers before him. Like them, he too dreams of living his entire life in the mountains. But his father puts an end to those dreams by sending him first to a boarding school, and then for a diploma in technical education to Bombay. On both occasions, he tried to convince his father against it, but his father refuses to be taken in by his arguments in the wake of large scale modernization and giant corporations wanting to take over the brand of cola marketed by the Kohlah family.

> Of course Mr. Kohlah refused the offer. For him it was not merely a business decision but a question of family name and honour.
>
> Besides, he was certain his good neighbours and the people of these settlements were not fickle; they would stay loyal to Kohlah's cola. He was prepared to put up a fair fight against the competition. [AFB – 268].

Upholding the generations old family name is of utmost importance to Farokh Kohlah as is ensuring a secure future for Maneck. But Maneck misunderstands his father and the rift between father and son gradually widens, ultimately leading to a deep abyss which does not get breached until their deaths. The ideal happy family of Maneck thus obruptly comes to an end.

To begin with, Maneck starts his life in Bombay in a hostel, where he undergoes the traumas of ragging, is befriended by the student leader, Avinash, and in the aftermath of the latter's mysterious disappearance from the hostel, driven to write a letter in desperation to his parents, pleading to be allowed to come back home to his family. At this juncture, his mother makes alterative arrangements for him to stay as a paying guest with her former school friend, Dina Dalal, nee Shroff.

Thus Mistry arranges a meeting point for the diverse strands created by him. The tailors after having searched in vain for suitable jobs for the six months they have been in the city are at last rewarded by jobs at Dina's. Maneck, on the point of taking a decision whether or not to stay on to complete the course, finds Dina's house as paying guest accommodation. This situation is aptly summed up by Bharucha.

> Thus the boy from the mountains meets the men from the village by the river and their lives become interdependent with that of the woman who lives in the city by the sea.[5]

From this point onwards, the destinies of the four main characters in the text are woven together by Mistry. They learn about each other's lives, learn to shed their differences and mix freely with each other, not only sharing their food, but also their joys and sorrows – all the components are necessary for a family to co-exist. For a family it is that Mistry describes in the chapter entitled 'Sailing Under One Flag'. The transition that takes place in their relationships, from employer – employee, to 'family members' is gradual. In the beginning there is a lot of mistrust on either side. Dina does not trust them enough and locks them in the flat when she goes to the export company to deliver the old order and get a fresh one. She also does not approve of Maneck's growing familiarity with Omprakash, who is approximately the same age. She voices her concern to Ishvar, whom she finds to be mature and more approachable.

> 'Nonsense'! She said that in her opinion, if it weren't for the uncle's steadying presence, Om would turn into a wastrel. 'I only hope he is not a poor influence on Maneck.' 'No no, don't worry. Om is not a bad boy. If sometimes he is disobedient or bad tempered, it's only because he is frustrated and unhappy. He has had a very unfortunate life.' ...
>
> From that day, he stayed behind more and more while Dina continued to make tea in Maneck's name but poured it in Ishvar's cup. They chatted about matters both tailoring and non-tailoring.
>
> Ishvar noted that the tea breaks upset Dinabai no more. It confirmed his suspicion, that she was longing for company. [AFB - 343].

Finding work and a place to stay, is not the end to all the troubles for Ishvar and Omprakash, though it is apparently so for the time being. Very soon, they return home only to find their rented, illegal accommodation being demolished. Without any place to go, they take refuge on the railway platform, only to be drenched with a bucket of cold water, as punishment for refusing to pay the policeman on duty. They hunt around for another place and the next night are rewarded with a little space in the entrance way of a chemist's shop in lieu of three rupees per night paid to the night watchman on duty. But carrying the heavy trunk to and from Dinabai's house each day, give him a sore left arm, which takes away her resolve of not getting too personal with the tailors. She massages some balm on the sore area herself.

> She uncapped the bottle. 'Come on, take off your shirt. What are you shy about? I'm old enough to be your mother.' He unbuttoned reluctantly. ... She dug a dark-green blob out of the bottle and started at the shoulder, spreading the cold unguent down towards the elbow in frigid one-finger lines. ... Then she began to massage. ... [AFB - 386].

This is another small, but significant step that Dina takes in overcoming the barriers of class and caste she is so conscious of. That evening she takes another step in showing the humane side to her nature by allowing the tailors to leave their heavy trunk in her flat, while they go to their place beside the chemist's shop to sleep for the night.

The tailors and Dinabai as a consequence have to go through some more hardships that are set by in store for them by Mistry. Orders are issued by concerned authorities to round up all beggars and send them to work in an irrigation project outside the city. The tailors are unfortunate enough to be forcibly picked up along with the beggars. They disappear for weeks together, without a word to Dinabai, who has no inkling of their whereabouts. Many weeks later, they turn up in a haggard state in the company of Beggar-master. Dina's immense relief is writ clearly in her words and in her face and she makes no efforts to disguise them either. At last she does the inevitable – offering them a place to sleep on her verandah.

From then onwards, its only a story of adjustments to each other's needs and learning from each other's habits. They discuss the benefits of toothpaste used by Dina to char coal powder and neem sticks, used by the tailors and decide in favour of the latter. The tailors easily adjust to Dinabai's routine of getting up early in the morning, finishing of their bath etc. well within schedule, maintaining immaculate cleanliness.

> The pattern of each day, thought Dina at the end of the first week, was like the pattern of a well-cut dress, the four of them fitting together without having to tug or pull to make the edges meet. The seams were straight and neat. [AFB - 476].

Soon Dina is so moved by the tailors' sense of gratitude and wanting to help in whatever capacity they can, that she decides to do away with all the reservations she has. The cups that she has kept separately for the tailors so far are not kept that way anymore-rather she takes to drinking in them herself. By and by they start eating together at the flat, occasionally with the tailors cooking their special recipes.

> Over the weeks, the tailors expanded their contribution from chapattis, puris, and wadas to vegetarian dishes like paneer masala, shak bhaji, aloo masala. There were always four people, or at least two, bustling about the kitchen in the evening. My bleakest hour, thought Dina, has now become the happiest. [AFB - 492].

Matters in Dina's flat seem to be proceeding at a happy pace and set routine. The tailors work vigorously at their sewing machines throughout the day, help out in the kitchen with the evening meals and then eat together as one happy family. One day, however, Ibrahim, the rent collector, witnesses the tailors at work and Maneck as well in the flat. Dinabai is quick to salvage the situation.

> 'You are talking rubbish!' she started the counterattack. 'This man, 'She said, pointing to Ishvar, 'he is my husband. The

> two boys are our sons. And the dresses are all mine. Part of my new 1975 wardrobe. Go, tell your landlord he has no case.' ... 'Tell your landlord, if he does not stop harassing my family. I'll take him straight to court!' [AFB - 505].

Some days later, however, the landlord's Goondas create problems for Dina, wrecking havoc in her flat, tearing, breaking and destroying everything in sight. Beggar-master comes to their rescue, as the tailors are his clients. He threatens the landlord and maims the men responsible for causing damage. For some time after this episode the family of four individuals – all from different walks of life have a smooth existence, until Ishvar decides to visit their village to get a wife for his nephew Om. At this juncture, the 'family' dissipates, leaving Dina alone in her flat to reminisce about the happy times. Savita Goel opines.

> The novel is not just a sordid drama of their lives, it is also about caring and sharing and the close relationship that the four characters gradually built up. Dina's kindly gestures of applying balm on Om's hand, permitting the tailors to sleep in her verandah after their traumatic experience, Maneck missing his college and helping Dina to complete the dresses, their idea of eating together and the friendly moments they spend together brightened their bleak lives[6]

The professional Beggar-master is depicted with a softer, emotional side to his nature with his accidentally discovering that the beggar whom he calls 'Worm' is actually his half – brother and the beggar-woman whose face looks hideous because of a gaping hole in place of a nose, therefore called Nosey, is his step-mother. The sudden discovery of a family he never knew to be possible has him over whelmed. He does everything in his power to make Nosey's death comfortable and lavishes affection and goodies on Shankar – 'Worm'. The extra attention that he is not used to has Shankar throwing a tantrum, ultimately leading to his death. The joy of possessing a family for Beggar-master is thus short-lived.

Mistry's second novel, thus, proves to be a saga of unlikely individuals grouped together to form families. The author seems to draw attention to the fact that a family does not have to consist of the regular set-up of grandparents, parents and children. In India it is a social custom to refer to a father's friend as 'Chacha' – Uncle and also treat him with due respect as one.

Unlike his second novel, Mistry's third novel deals with a regular family and its matters, aptly titled *Family Matters.* At the helm of affairs, is Nariman Vakeel, a 79 year old Parsi widower. He lives in a large apartment, which was once elegant. The apartment, housed in Chateau Felicity is now in a more or less, dilapidated condition. He lives with his two middle-aged, unmarried step-children, Coomy and Jal Contractor. His own daughter, Roxana, lives with her husband, Yezad Chinoy and two sons, Murad and Jehangir a small flat in Pleasant Villa.

Nariman has to depend on his step-children for the smooth functioning of his life. He loves to go out for his evening walks despite the several health problems he has. He refuses to be cowed down by Coomy's constant naggings and Jal's magnified fears regarding dangers of walking on the streets of Bombay. He retorts angrily:

> "Listen to me," he said, tired of waiting for calm to return to his limbs. "In my youth, my parents controlled me and destroyed those years. Thanks to them, I married your mother and wrecked my middle years. Now you want to torment my old age! I won't allow it." [FM - 7].

Nariman's angry retorts aptly sum up his unhappy life – how he has let the happiness of his life be ruined by bowing down to familial pressures. He had fallen in love with a Christian girl, Lucy, and wanted to marry her. But his father, an orthodox Parsi, refused to give in to his son's desires and stubbornly stood his ground. His father's friends then suggested the name of Yasmin Contractor, a widow, with two children Coomy and Jal. Nariman at that moment does not have the courage to oppose his parents' wish and forever repents that act of compliance. Lucy persistently tries to convince him otherwise, but he weekly gives in to the advice of his parents' friends:

> Now Mrs. Kotwal Scuttled across the room, pinched his check and said, "When the naughty boy at last becomes a good boy, it's a double delight."
>
> He felt like reminding her he was fortytwo years old. Then Nayesh Aunty beckoned from her seat on the sofa. 8...
>
> "No happiness is more lasting than the happiness that you get from fulfilling your parents' wishes. Remember that, Nari." [FM - 13].

Abiding by such advice, he had decided to get married to Yasmin, but had never been able to forget Lucy, which had been the main reason for his marital discord.

Coomy and Jal resent Nariman for not keeping their mother happy. They retain their name of Contractor, and Nariman does not object to it. The only happy memories all of them have of the turbulent years are of Roxana's birth.

> And if she could have remained that little baby for a while longer ? Perhaps that one period of his wedded life when he'd been truly happy might have lasted longer too. If only we could have the impossible, he thought, we could vanquish unhappiness. But that was not how things worked in the world. The joyous family time had been short. Much too short. [FM - 10].

Jal and Coomy are very devoted to their sister in her childhood. They look after her and take her everywhere with them. After their mother's tragic death, they shoulder the responsibility of bringing her up. On growing up, she decides to get married and opts to set up home elsewhere with her husband Yezad. Coomy and Jal cannot bring themselves to term with this and feel betrayed. Time and again she hints at this and on Nariman's birthday, lashes out at Roxana for gifting him with a walking stick.

> "The walking stick is a sign of how inconsiderate you've become. Never were you like this, nor till you got married and left. Now you have no concern for how we live or die. And that hurts me !"

> She turned away to dab of her eyes. Roxana watched for a few moments, feeling awful, then put her arm around her. "Come on, Coomy, don't be silly. Every day I think of you and Jal and Pappa. Please stop crying." [FM - 36].

Nariman has to put up with Coomy's bossing over things. She has laid down rules for nearly everything in the house. He has to announce his intention to use the W.C. He is not allowed to lock doors. On the occasions that he forgets the rules, he has to put up with a lot of ragging from Coomy. The only time he is happy is when Roxana visits with her family. He therefore excitedly anticipates the happy meeting on his birthday, and expectedly is sorry to see them go.

> The sad look of loneliness returned to Nariman's face, as Jal fetched the raincoats and umbrellas from the bathroom. Securiting the front door against the night, Coomy said that each time the Chenoy family visited, she felt exhausted, as though a whirlwind or a van olio had passed through.
>
> "That's strange," said Nariman. "To me it feels like a fresh breeze has stirred the stale air." [FM – 40-41].

Nariman, besotted with old age problems, osteoporosis, and Parkinson's disease, further complicates matters by accidentally falling into a trench. He now has to completely depend on Coomy and Jal ıor everything. They try to make things comfortable for him, yet Coomy cannot keep the resentment out of her voice and actions sometimes. The doctors had emphasized the point that Nariman was to be on complete bed rest, with no strain on his ankle. The first mistake Coomy makes is to buy a Commode for him. Jal and Coomy have a tough time putting their stepfather on the Commode and taking him off. His ankle gets terribly hurt in the process. Nariman feels very helpless and cries quietly at night. His step-children also cannot bear the brunt of the labour any more. Coomy argues with Jal that since Nariman didn't have to change her diapers as a child, she too isn't obliged to clean his bum and that it should actually be done by Roxana, his 'own flesh and blood, not like Jal and me, second class. "[FM - 7].

Jal as usual lets himself be convinced by Coomy and they prepare to literally dump Nariman into Roxana's house, without notice, unceremoniously.

Mistry paints a very happy picture of Roxana's family life in Pleasant Villa. A typical early morning, busy schedule is described, with Roxana among other things coaxing Jehangir to take his bath, while he tries to avoid doing it. The boys witness a tender moment pass between their parents and are happy, for on other occasions fights cloud over their time together. The two boys and Yezad prepare for their school and office respectively. Jehangir is detected with a mild stomach upset by Roxana and advised to rest at home. Roxana proceeds with the day's work and at this juncture the tranquility of the morning is broken with the unheralded arrival of Nariman on a stretcher, brought in an ambulance by Coomy and Jal.

Roxana tries her best to convince Coomy that looking after their old father in his present condition in her small flat would be next to impossible. But Coomy does not relent; sort of emotionally black mails her and departs with Jal leaving Nariman with his suitcase, medicines and bedpan with Roxana. Roxana tries to make the most of the situation, makes her father comfortable on the settee, changes his clothes and serves lunch to her son and father. Jehangir is overjoyed to see his grandfather and wants to feed him. They allow him to do so after he has finished his own plate. Watching the scene from the balcony, Roxana is over whelmed.

> The balcony door framed the scene : nine-year-old happily feeding seventy-nine. And then it struck her like a revelation – of what, she could not say ... she knew instinctively that it would become a memory to cherish, to recall in difficult times when she needed strength.
>
> Jehangir filled the spoon again and raised if to his grandfather's lips. A grain of rice strayed, lingering at the corner of his month. Jehangir took the napkin to gently retrieve it before it fell.
>
> And for a brief instant, Roxana felt she understood the meaning of if all, of birth and life and death. My son, she

> thought, my father, and the food I cooked. ... A lump came to her throat; she swallowed. [FM - 113].

This is a very touching portrayal of a scene immensely valuable in depicting human relationships. These are the moments Nariman longed for in the large flat at Chateau Felicity, where he silently wept at night feeling the rejection of his step-children. In the constrained space of the tiny flat at Roxana's he gets all the love and attention he could have wished for. He gets the feeling of being loved, and wanted, the sense of belonging to a family. Yezad is angry with Coomy and Jal for behaving abominably, for thoughtlessly pushing Nariman out of his own flat and advices Nariman to put his foot down. To this, Nariman replies as the mouthpiece of Mistry:

> "If I could put my foot down, everything would be fine." said Nariman with a wry smile. "How can you force people? Can caring and concern be made compulsory ? Either it resides in the heart, or nowhere." [FM - 121].

So in *Family Matters* , the Chinoy family with abundance of natural care and concern residing in their hearts, fight on valiantly with life's trials and tribulations to make matters easy for their family. Nilufer Bharucha opines:

> So the Chinoy family struggles on to care for Nariman and as the monthly budget becomes more and more strained, Roxana's men, each in his own way, attempts to supplement the dwindling pile of currency notes in the envelopes she has so painstakingly marked, butter, eggs, etc. and through which she tries desperately to juggle her monthly budget.[7]

Roxana constantly worries about Murad returning home late from school and the excuse offered by him is that he has missed the school bus. What is later revealed to the readers is that he has been deliberately walking home from school in order to buy Christmas gifts for his younger brother Jehangir, who he feels has been worrying too much lately about family finances. Yezad observes Murad putting the gifts in the stocking fashioned out of an old shopping bag by Roxana, which now hangs beside Jehangir's bed. Jehangir also watches Mukad but doesn't surprise him in the act. Yezad is overwhelmed by their brotherly love and mature thinking:

> He wanted to hug him, hug them both, tell them he loved them beyond measure, tell them now fortunate he was to have them for his sons, and how blessed they were to be brothers who cared about each other, and he wished their caring would never end, they would look out for each other all their lives. He wanted to wake Roxana, wake the chief, proclaim to everyone how he felt... [FM - 374].

Jehangir, in a bid to help his mother with the family budget, resorts to some dishonesty. He has been appointed Homework Monitor by his Class Teacher to check whether homework has been done properly. Jehangir takes the opportunity to make some money from the rich and not so intelligent boys in the class by marking their presentations satisfactory when it is far from so. The money made is discreetly slipped into his mother's envelopes. Shobhana Bhattacharji has this to say of the situation Jehangir is in.

> But *Family Matters* is about the life of the Vakee! family as well of their times. As he did in *Such a Long Journey* and *A Fne Balance*, in *Family Matters,* too, he places the microcosm of individuals' lives within the macrocosmic events. This time it is Bombay terrorized by the Shiv Sena. From the Vakeel family's small jokes about it, to its hosting the Michael Jackson concert, to the catastrophe in Yezad's life, the Shiv Sena permeates everything. Mistry never once mitigates the seriousness of its threat to civilized existence. He is conscious, too, of the insidious ways in which it can influence the smallest life (Young Jehangir, as homework monitor – an extraordinary concept in itself – accepts bribes for a "good cause", paralleling the protection rackets of the Shiv Sena).[8]

Yezad goes in for bigger money through the illegal Matka – Something he had made fun of in the past. His initial wins lead him to take bigger risks, until one day he empties all of Roxana's envelopes of their contents and bets it. Luck is not on his side and Matka is closed down by police and all the king pins put behind bars. Yezad is suddenly rendered without money. In his bid to help increase the dwindling family finances, Yazad does the opposite and confesses the entire episode to his wife, who though angry at first, learns to look at the positive side of things, of her husband again behaving in a rational manner. The situation in the Chenoy household is aptly described by Mistry in an interview with John Bemrose:

> Saddled by the cost of drugs to treat the old man's Parkinson's disease, his care taker's are only a few rupees away from unimaginable poverty. "There are millions and millions who live like that, "Mistry notes. "They don't think in terms of next year or next vacation. They think in terms of what they're going to cook for tonight's dinner."[9]

Through the various problems faced by the Chenoy family in looking after the ailing Nariman, issues close to Mistry's heart are discussed in detail. Roxana is happy for the exposure her sons are getting in caring for the aged. The young Jehangir, sleeping beside his grandfather in their small flat, is quick to hold his hand and comfort him when the latter has nightmares. Yezad, too, with his initial revulsion in handling Nariman's bed pan, and for bidding his sons from doing it as well, displays a massive shift in attitude. On an occasion when Roxana is not present in the house, Yezad surprises his sons by deciding to give the bed pan to Nariman who needs to do Number two. Between father and sons, they heave and heft and somehow manage successfully. Roxana returns when they are on the verge of completion – she is as much astonished as touched by the sight which meets her eyes.

> "Oh Pappa, no!" she cried from the hallway where the smell reaches her. "Did you spoil the bed ?" She entered the front room, saw them around the settee, the rags in Yezad's hand, and understood. "Thank you," she whispered, relieving him of the basket.
>
> "I'll do that."

"Thank Jehangir and Murad. Without them I could have done nothing." She smiled, and her eyes struggled to keep back the tears.

"I don't know how you manage alone," said Yezad.

'It isn't hard. With practice I've got used to it.

Not practice, he thought, love and devotion. Must be some truth in the saying that love could move mountains, it certainly let Roxana lift her father. [FM – 433 - 434].

This is another incident of the family's rallying together in adverse circumstances. Mistry seems to be saying this is what families are for. People joyfully share happy moments together, but when it comes to the sad, trying ones, are they as willing? Stacey Gibson comments.

"Nariman and his family could be plunked down in Bagonic, Sask., or Mont – Royal, Qre., and their struggles, their love for one another, their fallibilities, would resonate just as deeply."[10].

Mistry's third novel, *Family Matters*, could also be read in the light of the 'Lear Theme'. Nariman Vakeel is a professor of English and teaches college students. After the marriage of Roxana, he gifts her a flat at Pleasant Villa. Coomy and Jal, his step children, are very much upset with this action of his. To make them feel at ease, he writes the flat they stay in now, at Chateau Felicity, in their names. For the time being, everything seems to be all right. Things start going wrong when he breaks his ankle in an accidental fall. Coomy and Jal try looking after him in bed, but soon grow sick and tired of the entire procedure. Coomy convinces Jal that the best possible way is to let Roxana care for her father. They plan to take Nariman to her flat without prior information. When Nariman is consulted on this, he is non- committal.

Suppose I say no, thought Nariman, and give them good reasons- they could still have their way. Suppose I say yes, this flat is my home, and I put it in your names because I did not differentiate between you and Roxana. Would you now throw me out in my helplessness? They would Probably that think that I was getting dramatic. [FM -87]

Nariman feels helpless that the children he trusted so much are now behaving in such an abominable manner. Coomy and Jal take him to their sister's flat and leave him in an uncomfortable state of mind. Aftere some days they conspire to keep him away for a longer time. Coomy gets Jal to damage the roofs and walls of the house and pretend that the water tank overhead had leaked. When Roxana and Yezad go to check for themselves the extent of the damage, Coomy is very rude to them. They come back and report the matter to Nariman, who feels very foolish.

> "To so many classes I taught *Lear*, learning nothing myself. What kind of teacher is that, as foolish at the end of his life as at the beginning?" "What is *Lear*, asked Jehangir. Nariman swallowed the potato. 'It's the name of a king who made many mistskes." [FM -197]

Mistry seems to equate the life of Nariman to Shakespeare's *King Lear*. Nariman meets with the same fate as that of Lear in *King Lear.* The children Nariman trusted so much are unkind to him in his old age. He feels as foolish as Lear must have felt when he was treated badly by Reagan and Goneril. He had put his flat in his step children's names so that they don't feel bad, but they returned his kindness with unkindness. Nilufer Bharucha however argues that Coomy cannot be equated to Lear's unkind daughters as she had made an honest attempt to take care of her step- father, but had to take the extreme step because she was helpless.

REFERENCES

1. N.S. Dharan, 'Ethnic Atrophy Syndrome in Rohinton Mistry's Fiction', *Parsi Fiction,* Eds. Novy Kapadia, J. Dodiya and R. K. Dhawan, Prestige Books, Delhi, 2001.
2. Amritjit Singh,"Rohinton Mistry (1952)" Writers of the Indian Diaspora: A Bio- Bibliographical Critical Source. Nelson Emmanuel S(Ed.) Connecticut: Green Wood Press, 1993.
3. Ragini Ramachandra,. 'Rohinton Mistry's *Such a Long Journey: Some First Impressions', *Literary Criterion,* Vol. XXIX, No. 4, 1994.
4. Guy Lawson, *A Fine Balance, Mcleans,* Canada, 1996.

5. Nilufer E. Bharucha, *Rohinton Mistry: Ethnic Enclosures and Transcultural Spaces,* Jaipur : Rawat Publications, 2003. p. 157
6. Savita Goel, 'A Literary Voyage to India : Rohinton Mistry's *A Fine Balance',* in Jasbir Jain, *Writers of Indian Diaspore* : *Theory and Practice,* Jaipur : Rawat Publications, 1998, p. 196
7. Nilufer E. Bharucha.
8. Shobhana Bhattacharji, 'Remembered Time' Rev. of Family Matters. Pp 45-46.
9. John Bemrose, ' Salaam Bombay: Rohinton Mistry Again Recreates his Birthplace', Maclean's April 22, 2002.
10. Stacey Gibson, 'Such a Long Journey', *University of Toronto Magazine,* Summer 2002.

5

Discordant Feminine Voices in Mistry's Novels

The novels of Rohinton Mistry are accomplished works of art into which are woven elements of myth, history, fiction, knowledge about the Parsi Community, Indian politics and the city of Bombay in a rich and varied tapestry. As has already been noted in the previous chapter, the macrocosmic events have a direct bearing on the microcosm consisting of ordinary human beings belonging to the middle class and underprivileged sections of society.

The depiction of ordinary human beings necessarily means a great importance being laid on characterization by the author. In this chapter, I propose to examine the theme of 'Discordant Feminine Voices in Mistry's Novels' in the novels of Mistry. It would be appropriate to state Gordon Ekelund's views on the subject at the outset:

> Mistry clearly casts his women characters as one of two types in a dichotomy that defines women as either pure and silent – suffering, or malevolent – Pativratas or treacherous wenches. This dichotomy transcends cultural boundaries and is strongly entrenched in Indian tradition.[1]

The first female character that comes to mind in Mistry's first novel, *Such a Long Journey* is that of Dilnavaz. The readers are introduced to her as the wife of Gustad which is a very poignant statement. Gustad is not presented as Dilnavaz's husband. This attitude of Mistry speaks volumes. A women is known not in her own capacity, but in her relationship to a man. Dilnavaz possesses all the wifely virtues that one can name and ask for. She bothers about all the family members. Her sole aim in life is to keep the entire family happy. She is up and about at daybreak to fill water, make tea for Gustad, and buy milk.

> At water-tap time Dilnavaz awoke automatically, and her first thoughts were about Gustad and Sohrab. The terrible, terrible things they had said to each other. Exhausted, she stumbled sleepily to the bathroom. Water, water. Drums to fill. Hurry, kitchen tank to fill. That big bucket. And milk to buy ... [SaLJ – 62].

Along with her regular domestic chores, she is also worried about the terrible fight that had taken place between her husband Gustad and eldest child, Sohrab the night before. The occasion had been the ninth birthday celebration of their daughter, Roshan. Gustad had wanted to propose a toast to Sohrab's successfully clearing the IIT entrance exam. Sohrab in an uncharacteristic outburst, proclaimed that he was not interested in studying in IIT, although he had cleared the entrance. After the single invited guest had departed, Gustad had resorted to whipping Sohrab. But Dilnavaz, expectedly had intervened, only to receive a whiplash herself. The bitterness had remained unresolved at night, leading to Dilnavaz's worried thoughts in the morning. The courage with which she steps between an angry whip-wielding Gustad and an unrepentant Sohrab is praiseworthy. Gordon Ekelund, however, has other opinions :

> The woman is virtually numb, devoid of feelings and of ego. Her selflessness resembles the kind of disassociation often experienced by battered wives, an avenue certainly worthy of conscious exploration on Mistry's part, given that in the confrontation between Gustad and Sohrab, she is the one who limps away with welts on her legs.[2]

Ekelund, it seems is not very appreciative of this self-sacrificing nature of Dilnavaz.

To set matters right between Gustad and Sohrab, Dilnavaz resorts to black magic under the 'able' guidance of Miss. Kutpitia. She takes great pains to carryout Miss Kutpitia's instructions to the latter. Ekelund argues that. If we expunged all of Dilnavaz's forays into superstition from the novel, the plot would remain intact.'[3] He contrasts the several superstitious acts of Dilnavaz with the single one of Gustad's going to the Shrine of Mount Mary to pray for Dinshawji, Sohrab and Roshan. As a result of Gustad's absence from hospital on that fateful day, Dinshawji dies a lonely death, with nobody beside him. Mistry once again comes under criticism for giving importance to the actions of the male members as against the females. The only decisions Dilnavaz takes without her husband's knowledge and sanction are not given much importance. It almost seems as if the novelist indulges a mother's ego to do something worthwhile for her children.

Dilnavaz is not only hardworking, but is a tireless nurse as well. When Gustad has an accident, she meticulously follows the instructions given by Madhiwalla Bonesetter on alternative medicine, grinding the bark of a tree to obtain the paste to be applied, etc. This was in spite of the fact that Roshan was an infant being nursed by Dilnavaz in those days. With the same devotion she looks after Roshan too, when she is in bed with a chronic diarrhoea. The only difference this time being the medicines were supplemented with magic spells and rituals as suggested by Miss. Kutpitia.

Gordon Ekelund again criticizes Mistry for making a lot of show of the way Gustad 'Shares' everything important with Dilnavaz. The only news he holds back is the arrival of a letter from Major Bilimoria. But when the letter is found by Sohrab and read by his mother, does Dilnavaz's opinion matter ? In reality, Gustad's sharing only means, in other words, his telling her of something already decided by him or in the decision making process. Her opinions actually have no value whatsoever.

Nilufar Bharucha thus summarises the situation of Dilnavaz:

> Soul-destroying, mindless drudgery is the destiny of Dilnavaz in Rohinton Mistry's first novel, *Such a Long Journey.* Dilnavaz hovers at the periphery of the novel as her domestic crisis assumes national importance. Her husband-the man – is an active participant in this crisis but she is the hapless spectator.[4]

Dilnavaz's daughter, Roshan, has also been created by Mistry in her mother's reflection. She is delicate, fragile, sickly, gets frightened easily, and needs to be comforted and petted by her strong father. She is directly contrasted to her brothers Darius and Sohrab. She is physically weak in comparison to the well built appearance of Darius. As compared to Sohrab, she drastically falls short of his mental prowess. She does not have many aspirations, nor does she indulge in any hobbies. The only occasion that she talks of the future is when she is afraid of going to Dadaji- the fear instilled by the Knowledge of Dinshawji's death. Her fears are immediately put to rest by her father, who is quick to reassure her:

> Roshan considered this gravely. 'But I'm also very sick. When will I go to Dadaji?' What idiotic – lunatic talk ! Gustad used the phrase of anger to mask his dread. 'You are not very sick, you are much better. First you will grow up and get married, have children. Then they will marry and have their children, and you will be an old, old dossi before Dadaji is interested in calling you to heaven ! He looked at Dilnavaz reproachfully... [SaLJ-236].

Expectedly, Roshan does not question her father's statements. But the reader night very well find this ironic in that Gustad dreams of his eldest child joining the IIT and thus becoming successful in life. He is also happy to see Darius interested in body building and carpentry and is rather proud to see him use his great grandfather's hammer. His dreams for his daughter, Roshan, are to grow up, marry, and have children and naturally grow old. The reader feels this is just a stereotyping of character, noting interesting happening here.

Another important aspect worth mentioning about Roshan's characters is the ease with which she achieves everything in life. She gets them so easily, that achievement it is seems not to be the right word for them. She has to collect newspapers as a part of a drive initiated by her school. But wonder of wonders, she is handed a whole stack full of newspapers that she finds difficult to carry, by Miss. Kutpitia, without even having to ask for them. She desires to have a doll, and what a big doll she wins in the school lottery. Gordon Ekelund comments :

> Mistry's depiction of Roshan is typical of the portrayal of women in *Such a Long Journey.* Life happens to women, they are the object of masculine attention and desire. Character 'development' is inordinately based on physical description, and women are portrayed as 'types' rather than individuals.[5]

Miss Kutpitia, is the 'ubiquitous witch of fairy stories come to life'. She is symbolic of the Parsi, unmarried woman, who ends up with a much frustrated life. Her life story is reminiscent of Miss Havisham in Dickens' *Great Expectations.* She had taken the decision to remain unmarried on the day her brother's wife had died while giving birth to her nephew, Farad. With great love and affection, she had sacrificed her own desires in bringing up Farad. But fate does not want her to remain happy. Both Farad and his father are killed in a ghastly accident while returning from Khandala, leaving Miss. Kutpitia to lead an utterly lonely existence. From that day on, she has drawn into a shell of her own, with virtually no contact with the outside world. She is rather seen in the role of advisor to Dilnavaz, imparting her knowledge of various spells and rituals, which are supposed to 'cure' Roshan's chronic diarrhoea, and drive away the 'wrong' kind of thoughts from Sohrab's mind. Nilufer Bharucha feels.

> Instead her magic spells are reduced to being a mere manifestation of women's irrational nature. Mistry appears to be poking fun at this female behaviour. Miss. Kutpitia, being a spinster and a little batty is to be allowed her superstitions.[6]

Another interesting portrayal of female characters in *Such a Long Journey* is Alamai, Dinshawji's wife, who is always referred as 'my dear domestic vulture'. The initial stages of the novel has Mistry turning reader empathy away from her. She is portrayed as being neglectful of her husband's sexual needs, lazy enough to not send him fresh lunch with the dubbawalla, as is the custom with most others. Rather what is provided is the leftover from the previous night sandwiched between two slices of bread which her 'poor husband' has to necessarily eat. All these aspects have already been discussed in detail in the earlier chapter. A new light is thrown over this incident by Gordon Ekelund, which takes away some of the negative feelings readers may have developed towards her.

> Resisting the romantic overtures of a man afflicted by chronic halitosis may be as indicative of a well defined sense of self-preservation as it is of the vindictiveness Dinshawji insinuates. The pair are established as a classic comedy couple : a distinctly Parsi version of the shrew and her spouse the Laughable Lecher.[7]

Towards the end of the novel, however, Dinshawji's depiction of his wife rings true. Readers wait with Dinshawji in vain, to catch a glimpse of his wife who should have come hurrying. When Alamai does show up, it is with her nephew, Nusli, in tow. Nusli, although a young man, does not behave as one, and, Alamai constantly refers to him as the 'boy – without – brain'. She is more interested in having his trunk delivered back to her house than ensuring that his dead body is properly delivered to the Tower of Silence. She lives upto the label Mistry provides her – in the true style of a vulture she comes 'flying' only on sensing a waiting dead body.

The next female character who merits mention is the typist at the bank, Laurie Coutinuo. The reader is first introduced to Laurie as the target of Dinshawji's lewd jokes. He revels in making jokes at her expense in a language she does not understand – Gujarati. The other male colleagues enjoy such overtures and have justifiably named him the 'Casanova of Flora Fountain'. Dinshawji does his level best to live up to that image. He clowns around Laurie's desk and praises her for being ' not scared of my big, naughty snake', while she tries to not mind his jokes and take them in her stride.

> She smiled politely. Beads of perspiration were visible on Dinshawji's bald pate as the snake grew adventurous, moving with abandon into regions of daring proximity. Finally she said, 'I have so much typing to do. This place is always very busy, no?' [SaLJ - 98].

All through Dinshawji's jokes Gustad no doubt maintains a stoic silence, but the goings on in his mind, as revealed by Mistry speak of urges and desires similar to Dinshawji. He admires Laurie's patience and svelte figure'. His meeting with Laurie in a private room of a restaurant on the latter's request to discuss Dinshawji's jokes which have been carried too far *lately is utterly* illogical. The reader does not find Laurie's character easy to fathom. She does not want to talk to Gustad in everybody's hearing as she is bothered about her reputation. But the reader is kept in suspense which keeps building up with every step that Gustad takes with Laurie towards the private room, which 'spoke blatantly of the simple sordid purpose it was meant for. Laurie seems to be familiar with the purpose the room is used for, and inspite of the fact, does not feel uncomfortable. The reader on the other hand finds Gustad with all the uneasy feelings. This episode raises countless questions in the reader's mind, the most obvious being what kind of a girl is Laurie Coutino, and is Mistry taking readers for a ride by letting Lauries meet Gustad to complain about Dinshawji in a place which is far from respectable. The reader finds Laurie speak of decency in an indecent set up difficult to digest. Gordon Eklund's summing up of Laurie's character seems to be quite appropriate.

> Is Laurie a good girl or a bad girl, a Sita or a slut ? On one level, this type of 'is she or isn't she' game playing represents a failure to develop her character beyond the archetypal die into which all of the women in *Such a Long Journey* have been cast.[8]

Other minor female characters like Mrs. Rabadi and Mrs. Pastakia do not develop in the real sense of the word to merit discussion here. Mistry's portrayal of the women in the house of cages lacks authenticity being bereft of the dismal working conditions and the reason behind their being part of the reputed establishment.

At the heart of Mistry's second novel, *A Fine Balance,* is Dina Dalal, a Parsi widow. She is much concerned about the fact that in order to lead a life on her own terms, she must, somehow, maintain her economic independence. It is either this, or staying with her brother's family as a glorified domestic servant. The Prologue, very emphatically drives home this point.

> When Maneck left her flat, she began pacing the room, suddenly restless, as though about to embark on a long voyage. No need now to visit her brother and beg for next month's rent. She took a deep breath. Once again, her fragile independence was preserved. [AFB - 13].

That she does not want to live on her brother's charity is clear to readers. What has led to this unhappy situation becomes explicit in the first chapter, where Dina takes a walk down memory lane.

Readers are taken to Dina's childhood, when she is blissfully happy with a carefree life. Her father, a medical doctor by profession takes very good care of his children and does not let them want for anything. Dina, like Roshan in *Such a Long Journey,* is her father's pet. She, unlike her brother Nusswan, wants to follow in her father's footsteps and become a doctor. Her teachers and relatives predict a bright future for her. But the cruel hands of death snatch her father and her dreams, all in one go.

After maintaining a stoic exterior all through the funeral arrangements, her mother, Mrs. Shroff, suddenly withdraws into a cocoon, being lost to the external world. Without batting an eyelid, Nusswan is quick to assume charge of the household and the dispensary of Dr. Shroff. The latter is quickly sold off, and the former (household) is rendered short of staff on the plea that paying for so many of them was more than he could manage.

When Mrs. Shroff, his mother, expresses her doubts on the subject, as to who will do the all the work, etc. his reply is:

> "Don't worry, Mamma, we will all share it. You can do easy things, like dusting the furniture. We can wash our own cups and saucers, surely. And Dina is a young girl, full of energy. It will be good for her, teach her how to look after a home." [AFB - 21].

Dina does not agree easily to the new arrangement and is spiteful with Nusswan whenever the need arises. Nusswan time and again tries to make Dina obey his wishes – even whether she could get her hair cut not. He takes to beating her frequently in order to make her respect him. He takes her to the fire temple and asked her to pray properly.

> "Now pray properly – ask Dadaji to make you a good girl, ask him to make you obedient". [AFB – 24].

Mistry through these instances reminds us of the age old constructs of what goes into defining womanhood – docility, obedience 'being good', submissive, preparing from girlhood itself to look after a house in life. But through Dina's slow, but sure and spirited rebellion, he also brings hope to show that times are changing and all women do not take things lying down, without a murmur. Dina, with the help of her friend Zenobia, cuts off her hairs in school, even though it means a sound beating from Nusswan at home. From childhood itself Dina balances the tightrope, slowly, but effectively.

Dealing with Nusswan and fighting little battles and winning them or accepting defeat is not the only concern for Dina. She has to even think of ways and means of dodging the fingers of Dustoor Framji at the fire-temple.

> "This reputation for squeezing and fondlIng had earned him the title of Dustoor Daab - Chaab..." "Dina squirmed in his grasp as he patted her head, rubbed her neck, stroked her

back and pressed himself against her ... He released her just when she had summoned enough courage to tear her trapped body from his arms." [AFB - 23].

By and by, Dina devises ways of escaping the Parsi priest's lusty fingers. She merely extends a polite hand and takes a few steps back.

Dina's mother, Mrs. Shroff, who is from another generation does not match up in terms of perseverance and strength to her daughter. She lacks the mindset that resists life's unexpected tragedies. Her mental health visibly disintegrates after the sudden death of her husband. Shortly after Nusswan's marriage, she withdraws from life completely and does not respond to the instructions as before. About three and a half years of his father's death, she dies, finally succumbing to the intense grief at her husband's loss. Dina's aunt, 'Crazy Bapsy Aunty' follows in the steps of Mrs. Shroff, losing her reason after the loss of her spouse. For these women, being completely dependent on their husbands and never knowing liberty during marriage, the loss of their spouse is tantamount to the loss of a support necessary for living.

Shortly after his mother's death, Nusswan decides to discontinue Dina's schooling on account of bad performance, overlooking the fact that she does not get much time to study after completing household chores. Dina again protests and tries to rally support from her sister-in-law, Ruby, and their grandfather, very old and senile. But nothing works for her and eventually, she has to give up her schooling and be content with looking after his house. The resourceful Dina, however, finds ways of getting away from the drudgery. She saves money from the amount given by Ruby for shopping and uses it for the bus fare to visit the public libraries. Gradually her visits to these places increase and she educates herself in them, also making use of the music rooms in the more modern libraries. She also starts frequenting musical concerts where one was not required to buy a ticket.

It is at one such concert that she meets Rustom, her future husband. They keep meeting each other and eventually decide to marry. Nusswan, however, does not take her decision to marry an unassuming pharmaceutical chemist kindly. But Dina is determined and happy that once again she has been able to thwart her brother's plans for getting her married to one of his friends. She is able to preserve her dignity and shifts to Rustom's small flat after their marriage. Her marriage to Rustom is short but happy. He dies in a ghastly accident on their third wedding anniversary. Once again she has to take refuge in her brother's flat. But after a year of Rustom's death, Nusswan again starts introducing young men for her to marry. He firmly believes that she, being a woman needs male support to live and would go crazy like Bapsy Aunty if she did not marry. He further says:

> "Do you know how fortunate you are in our community? Among the unenlightened, widows are thrown away like garbage. If you were a Hindu in the old days you would have had to be a good little sati and leap onto your husband's funeral pyre, be roasted with him." [63 - 64].

Though Rustom's ghost continues to haunt her, she refuses to give in to Nusswan's sarcastic comments and goes back to Rustom's flat holding her head high. There she works as a tailor for some time somehow eking a living. But her eyes grow weak and with Zenobia's help and advice arranges for two tailors Ishwar and Om Prakash Darji to work for her in her flat and also takes in a paying guest, Maneck Kohlah, son of her former school friend. Once again Dina is able to preserve her 'fragile independence' (13) as observed by the author in The Prologue, and not approach Nusswan for the rent of the flat.

The narrative shifts back and forth in time. We are informed how Dina undergoes many more trials and tribulations. The tailors being male try to outsmart her, but she holds her own. There are constant threats from the rent collector which also she survives. What she cannot survive, however is unforeseen circumstances which take Maneck and the tailors away from her life. Maneck goes to Dubai with a job and the tailors go to their village to find a bride for Om. Once there, they fall victim to the caste oppression they left behind and also enforced vasectomy in the government's twenty point programme. Gangrene destroys Ishwar's legs and they are finally amputated. Om is also castrated and his testicles removed. Thus maimed, they return to the city of Bombay (not named directly in the novel) and to Dinabai. Dina by now has been forced to go back to her brother's as a glorified servant. But even there she surreptitiously keeps helping her tailors – turned beggars by feeding them in her brother's best china behind his back. This is her final show of independence as also of maintaining a 'fine balance' between hope and adversity. She has come full circle in her journey of life.

Dina's counterpart in the village by the river exists in the form of Dukhi Mochi's wife Roopa. Roopa also falls in the archetypal role of the mother who lavishes special care and affection on the male child. When a son is born to Roopa after three daughters who die in infancy, she is extra vigilant about him.

> The child was called Ishvar, and Roopa watched over him with the special ardour and devotion she had learned was reserved for male children. She made sure he always had enough to eat ... But for this child she did not hesitate to steal either...
>
> After her milk went dry, Roopa began nocturnal visits to the cows of various landowners...
>
> She took only a little from each cow; thus, the owner would not sense a decrease in the yield. When Dukhi saw the milk in the morning, he understood.
>
> If he awoke in the night as she was leaving, he said nothing, and lay shivering till she returned...
>
> Soon... Roopa began to pay weekly visits to orchards in season and ready for harvest. [AFB - 118].

The passage quoted above raises some pertinent aspects pertaining to the portrayal of women in Mistry's fiction.

This is the only occasion in the three novels where Mistry discusses lives of non-Parsi women in minute detail. The beginning of the passage refers to the age – old constructs where mothers often distinguish and differentiate between male and female children. The first three daughters of Roopa die in infancy. The reader might question – do the infants die a natural death or are they willed to die through gross neglect ? Why are they not recipients of the 'ardour and devotion' reserved for male children ? will the mother, known for her inexhaustible wealth of love for her children, find it suddenly diminishing if showered lavishly on the girl child ?

For the sake of her 'male' child, Roopa takes to stealing milk from cows and fruits from orchards in the dead of night, lest the child should want for anything. The reader marvels at the courage displayed by Roopa and the extent to which she is ready to take risks for the well – being of her child. Never does she pause to consider the tremendous risk her nocturnal visits entail. On one such mission, tables are turned upon her, in the form of a night watchman who catches her red-handed. The worst happens and Roopa is raped by the man. She bears it all silently for the sake of her child. How much ignominy is a mother prepared to suffer for a male child ? What about the passive role played by Dukhi in the entire drama ? How can he lie there feigning sleep and pretend as if things are normal in the morning ? Or is the reader to understand that Dukhi Mochi is the symbol of the poor passive male who cannot help but wait endlessly for things to happen, powerless to make things happen and change the course of events. Mistry seems to be saying that when the supposedly strong' male is rendered helpless in the face of circumstances, it is the supposedly 'weak' female who dares to defy them and make the best of available resources.

Another case of gender discrimination is evident in the way Narayan's son, Omprakash, and his daughters, Leela and Rekha, are treated differently by the older women. This refers to the time when Omprakash, staying with his uncle, Ishvar, to learn tailoring in the town. Whenever he comes home in between, he is fussed over by his mother, Radha, and grandmother, Roopa.

> Omprakash's sisters resented his visits. No one paid attention to Leela and Rekha if their brother was in the house. It started as soon as he stepped in the door.
>
> 'Look at my child ! How thin he has become !' complained Radha. 'Is your uncle feeding you or not ?' ...
>
> But she used the excuse to lavish on him special treats like cream, dry fruits, and sweetmeats, bursting with pleasure while he ate ...
>
> Roopa, too, relished the sight of her lunching, munching grandson. She sat like a referee, reaching to wipe away a crumb from the corner of his month, refilling his plate, pushing a glass of lussi within his reach ... [AFB - 173].

Amidst all this adulation for Omprakash, his sisters feel unjustly neglected and generally cry themselves to sleep at night, with nobody having the time to wipe away the tears. The tears shed by Leela and Rekha are shed by millions of such girls with a similar predicament in India.

Another burning social issue raised by Mistry is that of female infanticide. When two sons are born to Dukhi and Roopa, the news is not received happily by upper – caste families. They are beside themselves with jealousy.

> The news of a second son created envy in upper – caste homes where marriages had also taken place around the time Dukhi and Roopa were wed, but where the women were still childless or waiting a male issue. It was hard for them not to be resentful – the birth of daughters often brought them beatings from their husbands and their husbands' families. Sometimes they were ordered to discreetly get rid of the new born. Then they had no choice but to strangle the infant with her swaddling clothes, poison her, or let her starve to death. [AFB - 121].

Female foeticide and infanticide are much debated and written about issues in India. A very hot topic of discussion, the issue finds mention in the present novels of Mistry as well. This problem is so severe that it knows no barriers of caste and class. Members from all strata of society rejoice or grieve on the birth of a son or daughter respectively. Sons are so much in demand that families are prepared to go to any extent for the birth of a male heir, propitiating the gods, keeping difficult fasts, going on arduous pilgrimages, etc. The need for a male heir is so completely instilled in the minds of women, that women become the greatest enemies of their own sex, ready to abort without any qualms and kill if necessary the innocent little girls.

Mistry makes passing references to another social evil, that needs to be eradicated, quickly and surely that of bride burning and dowry deaths. The tailors, Ishvar and Om discuss future plans of the latter's marriage, when Dinabai, their employer, interposes :

> '... Remember, Om, treat your wife with respect. No shouting or screaming or beating. And one thing is certain, I will not allow any kerosene stoves on my verandah.'
>
> Ishvar understood her allusion, veiled though it was. He protested that bride burnings and dowry deaths happened among the greedy upper castes, his community did not do such things.
>
> 'Really? And what does you community say about male and female children ? Any preferences?' [AFB - 581].

Before this exchange of ideas about dowry deaths and bride burning, there is another discussion on the role of women in society, and the expectations from them as wives.

> 'It will be perfect, Dinabai, believe me. For all of us. She will be useful to you also. She can clean the house, go to the bazaar, cook for-'
>
> 'Are you getting a wife for Om, or a servant ?' she inquired, her tone caustic.
>
> 'No, no, not servant, 'he said reproachfully. 'Why does it make her a servant if she does her duties as a wife ? How else do people find happiness except in fulfilling their duty?'
>
> 'There can be no happiness without fairness,' she said. 'Remember that Om, - don't let anyone tell you otherwise.' [AFB - 578].

This outburst from Dina Dalal somewhat explains her past behaviour – as to why she chose to many Rustom Dalal, ignoring all the 'better' proposals suggested by her brother, why she chose to come away from her brother's place after a year's stay on becoming a widow, and why in a desperate bid she found the two tailors to work for her and took in Maneck as a paying guest. All her efforts are towards one goal to maintain her independence. As a young girl, her brother makes her slog all day at home, which she found unfair. She starts by registering her protest in various ways, to show that she is unhappy. Whenever she stays with her brother on a long term basis, he gets rid of the domestic help, implying that Dina is as good as one. Her words of advice to Om, about to get married, are suggestive of the kind of behaviour she would expect for herself – that 'there can be no happiness without fairness'.

It is possible that Mistry ends the novel on this note of fairness and happiness. When the tailors become beggars, they come to Dina's brother's house, where she is now forced to stay, for want of independent accommodation. To the best of her ability, Dina tries to help them by providing them with a decent lunch every day, served on her brother's best china. In a private conversation I had with Dr. Nilufer Bharucha, she commented that although Dina has a spirit to rebel, 'what and where is the result ? She is unable to get out of the clutches of cruel circumstances and fate'. I would like to mention here, that although Dina is not able to make her mark on the outside world, she is happy in the thought that she lets two beggars eat from the very plates used by Nusswan and his wife. For her this is a way of achieving happiness through fairness.

The other women in the novel, namely, Mrs. Shroff, Mrs. Aban Kohlah, Ruby, Zenobia, Mrs. Gupta and Shirin Aunty are all important to the development of the plot. They come across as characters who bring out either positive or negative qualities in the main characters. They come across as poor stereotypes of the archetypal image of the docile wife, with all the virtues that a good wife must possess, or a successful business – woman as in the case of Mrs. Gupta and Zenobia, who do not have to struggle to become so. These characters are not promising as far as development is concerned, and therefore do not merit place in the present discussion.

Mistry's third novel, *Family Matters,* has a host of women as characters who are somehow related to the pivotal figure of Nariman. The first one who needs to be mentioned is Lucy Braganza, a Goan Christian with whom Nariman Vakeel has a long drawn out affair, but unfortunately cannot marry. The reader is given an insight into the affair and the tragic ending to it through flashbacks of Nariman, who has now attained a ripe old age of seventy – nine. There were objections raised by the families of both Nariman and Lucy as neither of them wanted to compromise on their rather orthodox stand. Nariman ultimately had given in to parental pressure and agreed to marry a Parsi widow with two children. His decision to marry Yasmin wrecks hevoc on Lucy's mind who cannot reconcile herself to the fact. She tries her best to dissuade Nariman saying none of them would be happy with the marriage.

> ...Lucy tried one last time to convince him; they could turn their backs on everyone, walk away from the suffocating world of family tyrannies, from the guilt and blackmail that parents specialized in. They could start their own life together, just the two of them.
>
> Struggling to maintain his resolve, he told her they had discussed it all before, their families would hound them, no matter what. The only way to do this was to end it quickly. [FM – 13 - 14].

Nariman goes ahead with the plans for his marriage to Yasmin Contractor, who has considered a second marriage only for the sake of her children, Jal and Coomy. By this time, Lucy has been disowned by her parents and decides to do whatever she can in order to be as close to Nariman as is possible in the present circumstances. She pursues him outside his classes, and he in turn tries his best to avoid her. Later, she takes to standing on the pavement opposite his house staring at his window until he went down to meet her. Yasmin at first takes things lightly, advising Nariman on the best way to tell her off, without causing hurt. All her advices go unheeded, as Nariman is extremely gentle with her. Yasmin takes to applying stricter measures by hiding all his clothes on one occasion, with the objective of preventing Nariman from going to meet Lucy on the pavement. Nariman, however, goes down in a towel to tell Lucy that she should not behave in the present fashion, which caused suffering to all the others involved, however indirectly. Lucy then takes up a job as an ayah with the Arjanis, who stay on the ground floor of Chateau Felicity. By this time she starts behaving abnormally, by climbing on the ledge high above the terrace and singing songs, until Nariman went to meet her and coax her to come down.

The state of affairs in the Vakeel household are indeed sad with Yasmin threatening to desert her husband taking the three children (by this time Roxana has been born) along, if Nariman did not stop going to meet Lucy on the rooftop singing songs. Things reach a head with Yasmin deciding to take matters into her own hands and going to the roof top to tackle Lucy. Nariman follows her, but cannot stop the tragedy which takes place in front of his eyes – the two women accidentally fall from the rooftop to their deaths.

In this tragedy reader empathies are with Yasmin who comes across as a strong woman – more a strong mother, much dedicated to the well-being of her children (somewhat resonant of the character of Roopa in *A Fine Balance)*. Yasmin has remarried with the sole purpose of providing a good life to her children, which seems to be threatened with Nariman's affair. The tragedy on the rooftop is unfortunate, as it leaves her children desolate and bitter towards Nariman, holding him responsible for their mother's death. Lucy Braganza, on the other hand, loses the sympathy of the reader by her persistent efforts to keep meeting Nariman, not letting him forget for one moment their love affair. When two adults take a rational decision, it is expected that they would abide by it. In this case Lucy takes on negative shades by refusing to understand that Nariman now has a family to look after, and her behaviour only succeeds in ruining the family's happiness. She seems to be somewhat selfish – bent upon getting a little happiness for herself, but at what a terrible cost!

Coomy Contractor, Yasmin's daughter from her first marriage grows up from a resentful child to a bitter woman. She still retains happy memories from her childhood when her father, Palonji Contractor was still alive. On her mother's second marriage, she, along with her brother, Jal, insist on referring to Nariman as New Pappa. She is old enough to understand and remember the cause of bitterness in her mother's life. After her mother's death, she cannot forgive and forget what happened inspite of all that Nariman does to bring them up and provide them with all the necessities. Coomy has not married, is middle aged, and reminds readers of Miss. Kutpitia in *Such a Long Journey.* She is very fond of her little sister, Roxana, and in her childhood used to proudly carry her around like a doll, looking after all her needs on their mother's demise. She cannot come to terms with the fact that Roxana, on growing up, chose to marry and set up a separate house with husband Yezad. When Nariman lies in bed with a broken ankle, she resents having to look after him and grudges Roxana her good fortune of not having to go through it all by virtue of marriage.

After a few days of back breaking labour, she conspires with, and convinces Jal to shift the ailing Nariman to Roxana's flat, without prior notice. This conspiracy on Coomy's part is seen in negative shades by readers, but Bharucha is quick to defend her:

> While the reader might be tempted to censure Coomy for this 'heartless' move, her action needs to be seen against the earlier mentioned scenario where there is no state help at all for the care of the old and infirm and the entire burden falls upon their not always willing to do so children.[9]

The reader night tend to agree with the powerful agreement offered by Bharucha, but what excuse or defence can there be for Coomy, when she further plots to keep Nariman away from his own home ? She makes Jal get a heavy hammer from

Edul Munshi downstairs and severely damage the plaster on the roofs and wall of all except one room – the one which belonged to their dead mother. When Jal accuses her of haring ruined relations with Roxana forever, she (Coomy) suddenly gets sentimental.

> "Don't turn away ! You said you wanted a ruin, so feast your eyes ! Happy ? Ruined house, and ruined relations with our one and only sister.'
>
> Then his voice lost its hysterical edge, suddenly subdued by sorrow. Exhausted, he sank into a chair and covered his face. She sat too, watching him, thinking of all that he'd said, thinking of Roxana...
>
> Their little doll... how they had loved her when she was born, how crazy they were about her, carrying her everywhere, ... and how much she had adored them, in those childhood years ...
>
> What remained now of all that love ? ...
>
> "What's wrong?"
>
> "Nothing. "Then she began to weep. No one gave a thought to her feelings, she whispered, the unkind things they said to her, and Yezad a accusing her of stealing from Pappa, after all that she had done for Pappa, for so many years ... [FM 194].

The devastation started by Coomy reaches its climax with her death along with Edul Munshi, buried under the debris in Nariman's room, when the beams he has been trying to fix suddenly come crashing down. Inspector Masalavala comments:

> "Same goes for your sister. I don't mean to upset you, Jal, but if she had married, she would have been in her husband's house, far from the steel beam that broke her skull." [FM - 415].

This seems to be Mistry's comment on the sorry state of unmarried women in general and Parsi women in particular. His comment suggests that if these women marry at the right age, it is possible they would be happier and away from such avoidable disasters.

Roxana, the biological daughter of Nariman, has shades of Roshan in *Such a Long Journey.* The family looks forward to Roxana's visits with her husband and kids. She is likened to a doll in childhood whom everybody likes to pet and carry around, and like a precious possession nobody wants to let go of her. Coomy had wanted Roxana to live on in Chateau Felicity along with her husband after marriage – not wanting to relinquish her hold on her lovely doll, brought up almost like a dear daughter after their mother's death.

Roxana is an ideal daughter, wife and mother. She is concerned about her sons' health almost to the brink of obsession. She keeps a strict count on the number of times they have been to the wc, etc.

> But his mother was keeping count. "Third one ? what's wrong? And your brother has sneezed seven times since he woke up." [FM - 94].
>
> He sniffed his twice – washed fingers to make sure they carried the soap fragrance : Sometimes his mother demanded proof. But her inquiry now was about the stomach, not hands; she wanted to know if it was runny all three times, and was there any mucus.
>
> He hated these bowel questions, they embarrassed him, made him feel like an infant in diapers. Ignoring them was impossible, Mummy would keep pestering...
>
> "Second and third time runny, no mucus," he said in a monotone, and rejoined the breakfast table. [FM - 95].

Roxana worries about her husband's health and happiness at all times. She takes extra care to ensure that the mornings which he loves to enjoy with his family should be trouble free. In the evenings, she instructs her sons to behave themselves and finish off their studies so that when Daddy gets back from work, he finds things in order. She adores her husband, appreciates the amount of botheration he faces at work, and like the virtuous wife is determined to keep him happy at all costs.

> She watched him return to the fray, knowing how it would end in the evening, and knowing that he knew it too, and yet he persevered. Then she felt her husband was as brave and strong as any Rustom or Sohrab, her hero, whose mundane exploits deserved to be recorded in his very own Shah – Name, his Yezad – Nama, and she thanked fate, god, fortune, whoever was in charge.
>
> She feared about how Pappa's arrival would affect their morning. No matter what, she had to preserve its rhythm for Yezad. Yes, she was determined: not a hair of the routine that gave him so much joy would be allowed to change. [FM – 118 - 119].

She looks after her ailing father with all the care and concern he deserves. In between her tight morning schedule, she manages time to give him the urinal or the bedpan, whichever was required.

In striking contrast to the character of Roxana is Mrs. Kapur, who comes across as a very cold, calculative business woman operating from behind the scene. Mr. Kapur is very enthusiastic to contest the municipal elections in Bombay and has very idealistic feelings for the city. However, his enthusiasm is dampened by his wife's insistence that family comes before everything else and that he should know better than to squander the hard-earned money on the elections. On Mr. Kapur's death, Yezad is quite shocked at the quiet composure with which she conducts herself. She has kept a record to the last rupee of the money her husband has put by in the suitcase. Yezad is surprised to learn that she is not aware of the sentimental side to her husband's nature – how much the name Bombay meant to him. She even refuses to let Yezad take the three old photographs of Bombay that had been gifted to him by Mr. Kapur on Christmas day.

Through the contrasting examples of Roxana and Mrs. Kapur, Mistry seems to be upholding the role of the ideal, virtuous lady of the house. In all his three novels, he glorifies such characters – Dilnavaz in *Such a Long Journey,* Roopa in *A Fine Balance* and finally Roxana in *Family Matters.* These women come across as selfless, putting their family, husband, children above everything else. They are beautiful, soft weak and look up to the men for most things in life. It would be appropriate to use Gordon Ekelund's words here.

> An archetype without life is simply a stereotype. At times, the women in this novel seem reduced to mere plot devices, objects through which men reveal their character. We are left with a sense of incompleteness, of stories left untold, of avenues left unexplored. In *Such a Long Journey*, women and girls have been left at the station. An otherwise accomplished first novel is compromised by this structural flow.[10]

This analysis of portrayal of women in *Such a Long Journey* by Ekelund can be stretched to include Mistry's other novels as well. The women, whenever they try to protest, are brought back to seeking support from the men in their lives, unable to exist by themselves, in a world of their own- that privilege is reserved for the men in Mistry's novels.

This chapter deals with the Discordant Feminine Voices in Mistry's Novels'. It has been found through a close analysis that the female characters in Mistry's novels do not really come across as round characters. Mistry does not allow them to develop much. Rather they are cast as stereotypes. Dilnavaz, Dina, Roxana, are all beautiful women who are really concerned about their families. They are at times ready to sacrifice whatever they can in order to maintain peace in the family. Bharucha feels that the character of Daisy in *Family Matters* is the most promising one of all the women in Mistry's novels. She is the only one who has achieved much in her career without the support of a man- a commendable feat indeed. She has got the spirit to carry forward, achieving higher goals.

REFERENCES

1. Gordon Ekelund, "Left at the Station: The Portrayal of Women in Rohinton Mistry's *Such a Long Journey*", p. 7

2. *Ibid*. p. 11
3. *Ibid*. p. 12
4. 'From Behind a Fine Veil: A Feministic View of Three Parsi Novels', Margins of Erasure: Purdah in the Subcontinental Novel in English, Eds. Jasbir Jain & Amina Amin, Sterling Publishers Private Limited, Delhi, 1998.
5. Gordon Ekelund, p. 10.
6. Nilufer E. Bharucha, *Rohinton Mistry: Ethnic Enclosures and Transcultural Spaces,* Jaipur: Rawat Publications, 2003. p. 133.
7. Gordon Ekelund, p. 7.
8. *Ibid*. p. 9
9. Nilufer E. Bharucha, *Rohinton Mistry : Ethnic Enclosures and Transcultural Spaces,* Jaipur: Rawat Publications, 2003. p. 178.
10. Gordon Ekelund, p. 14.

6

Development of Themes

Rohinton Mistry's works, located as they are in diverse disciplines have achieved world wide acclaim. He is acknowledged as a major writer of the Indian Diaspora. As a Parsi Zoroastrian he has had to cope with multiple displacements, beginning with the original one from Iran. The preceding chapters of this study were attempts to explain his fictional work with respect to four largely recurrent themes – the Parsi Environment in India, Bombay as background, Matters of the Family, and Discordant feminine voices. The present chapter aims to analyze how these themes are realized in his work – what are the techniques employed, and what are the major motifs used.

If *Don Quixote* and *Joseph Andrews* belong to the picaresque tradition, Rohinton Mistry's award winning novel of the road, *Such a Long Journey* (1991) is obviously not of the picaresque mode. In Mistry's novel spatial and temporal paths of the most varied people intersect, which leads to collapse of social distance, passage through familiar territory, and revelation of socio-historical heterogeneity of one's own country. Yet the difference from the Cervantean mode is what distinguishes the novel and makes in unique.[1]

(A) Motif of Journey/Quest

The motif of journey is of central concern to most writers of the Indian Diaspora. In *Such a Long Journey,* there are three epigraphs which introduce this motif. The first is from Firdausi's Iranian epic *Shah Nama,* which recalls the glorious Iranian heritage and the conditions of the present day Parsis in its downgraded condition. The second epigraph from T.S. Eliot's *Journey of the Magi* is reminiscent of the ancient Zoroastrian religion and the belief that the magi who attended the birth of Christ were in reality Zoroastrian priests. The epigraph from T. S. Eliot's poem is also responsible for the title of the novel *Such a Long Journey.* The third epigraph which is taken from Tagore's *Gitanjali* traces the journey of the Parsis from Iran to India and beyond. It also informs readers of the various ways in which the Parsis have consistently adapted themselves to the new circumstances.

The novel is about Gustad Noble and his family which consist of his wife Dilnavaz, two sons Sohrab and Darius and daughter Roshan. The family seems to be happy in itself until the major disturbance in the form of a letter from Major Bilimoria, requesting Gustad's help in a secret mission. Major Bilimoria had suddenly disappeared from Khodadad Building, about a year ago without informing his best friend. This incident refers to the Nagarwala incident, involving a Parsi in a very 'shameful' act. According to Nilufer Bhrucha,

> "In *Such a Long Journey* the Parsi world gradually moves out of its self-imposed isolation and interacts at the highest levels of finance and politics with the postcolonial Indian world."[2]

When Gustad decides to help the Major, he is advised against this by his wife and son Sohrab. But Gustad has already taken a decision. By this time he is also tremendously disappointed with Sohrab for not joining the IIT, even after clearing the entrance exam. Father and son have a misunderstanding, and Sohrab ultimately decides to leave his parents' house in protest. Thus begins his journey into the outside world of his own choice.

Gustad doesn't try to stop his son. In the meantime, Roshan falls seriously ill and Gustad has to journey several times to the doctor's clinic in order to get treatment for her. He meets his old friend Malcolm Saldanha, on one of his journeys to Crawford market of Bombay. He also has to visit the Chor Bazar of Bombay according to the letter received from the Major. He has been asked to deposit ten lakhs into his bank as a favour to the Major. In this endeavour he enlists the help of his colleague, Dinshawji. When they have deposited about half the money, they are ordered to withdraw it as soon as possible. Gustad learns from newspaper reports that the Major is in deep trouble in New Delhi. In a letter to Gustad, the Major requests him to come down to New Delhi to meet him. His friend, Gulam Mohammad, hands him a ticket to New Delhi to visit the Major. Gustad is not very keen to do so. The journey also enables Gustad to ponder, 'would this long journey be worth it? Was any journey worth the trouble?' [SaLJ – 259].

The railway journey to Delhi, enables Mistry to talk about the philosophical journey of life and its seriousness. In Delhi, however, Gustad meets his old friend, Major Bilimoria in a very pathetic condition in jail. All of Gustad's doubts are cleared by his friend and he leaves for Bombay with a peaceful mind. In this novel, Bharucha

> "feels the female characters in it do not journey at all. They remain stationary while the world around them moves and changes. Theirs is a static universe where they are denied knowledge of even their own stultification and repression by their creator."[3]

Another journey is undertaken by the pavement artist at the end of the novel, when the Wall of All Religions that he has so lovingly painted with Gods and Goddesses, is demolished by the municipal corporation. In reply to Gustad's question as to where he would go, he answers;

> 'In a world where roadsides become temples and shrines and temples and shrines become dust and ruin, does it matter where?' [SaLJ - 338].

Purvi Upadhyay, sums up the predicament of Gustad in Mistry's first novel in the following words,

> Like the journey of the Magi, Gustad's arduous trek through pain, heart break and loss has brought him to a new awakening and the promise of the ultimate victory of human spirit. Ultimately the novel *Such a Long Journey* celebrates through the metaphor of the journey the all inclusiveness of life and the indestructibility of the human spirit.[4]

In Mistry second novel, *A Fine Balance*, Dina Dalal, journeys from her brother's house to her husband's, back to her brother's on becoming a widow and again decides to go back to her dead husband's flat to live an independent life. In Bharucha's words,

> "She moves from protected girlhood under the indulgent care of her doctor father, to the harsh reality of reductive femaleness under the 'protection' of her brother Nusswan. Her awareness of her autonomous existence does not allow her to bow down to the patriarchy that Nusswan seeks to impose on her".[5]

Dukhi Mochi also makes a successful journey of sorts by daring to go against the higher caste Thakurs of his village by apprenticing his sons to a Muslim tailor in the town. His son, Narayan, also dares to offend the Thakur by wanting to caste his own vote. As a punishment for this, he is brutally tortured by the Thakur's men and killed along with his entire family. Ishvar and Omprakash journey to Bombay on the advice of their Ashraf Chacha as they are powerless to take any revenge against the mighty Thakur, and also to make a better life for themselves. After a lot of experiences, they journey back to their village to look for a bride for Om. The Thakur recognizes them and in the Nussbandi Mela that is going on in the village, they too are operated upon. The tailors now have become beggars and journey back to Bombay.

Maneck Kohlah, a boy from the mountains, journeys to the city to study in a better course. He comes across the tailors in Dinabai's house where he stays as a paying guest. After the course is over, he journeys back to the mountains, in search of happiness, can not find it, and then journeys to a Middle Eastern Country in search of a good pay packet. When he returns to Bombay, he finds everything has changed. He is not ready to change himself and commits suicide on the railway track. This is again a philosophical comment by Mistry on the journey of life.

In *Family Matters*, there are no significant, physical journeys that the characters undertake. In fact, they do not move out of the precincts of Bombay at all. At the most they go to each other's houses, their schools, office, the market, share bazaar, or to the Tower of Silence. The journey is rather psychological in nature, from past to present, from innocence to experience, of a more pan – universal appeal.

The journey of life in the cases of first Mr. Kapur, Coomy, Edul Munshi and lastly Nariman come to an end, in the real sense of the word. In the case of Nariman, it is a full life, living to a grand old age of eighty plus. In his lifetime he has seen many ups and downs. In his youth, he courts Lucy Braganza, which is not appreciated by his parents. He does not have the courage to stand up in opposition against them, marries Yasmin which is contrary to his wishes. Destiny plays its part, with Yasmin and Lucy both dying, leaving Nariman to care for the three children, Coomy, Jal, and Roxana. What follows is a life of bitterness for Coomy. She dies with a bitter heart, holding her step father responsible for their unhappy life.

Mr. Kapur and Edul Munshi die at quite a young age. Mr. Kapur, very idealistic of Bombay, had wanted to pump his life blood into it if required and that is what is taken from him. His words prove prophetic. He dies with many aspirations, unfulfilled. Edul Munshi has a penchant for being a handyman, tries his hand at carpentry, and much against the wishes of his wife, Manizeh, undertakes elaborate repairs at Nariman's flat at Chateau Felicity. Fate intervenes,

> As it came crashing down, it swept Edul off the ladder. Coomy tried to dodge, but the glancing blow on the head

> was enough to break her skull. The girder came to rest across Edul's chest where he lay upon the floor. [FM –395].

The two children of Roxana, Murad and Jahangir, grow up from children into young boys. They also become mature. The novel from their point of view can also be read as a journey from innocence to maturity. The Epilogue in Jahangir's voice informs the reader of the happenings in the family after they move into Chateau Felicity, having sold off their own flat at Pleasant Villa. Jahangir claims to remember everything that has happened since his grand father had come to stay with them in their tiny flat. He has become quite mature. He shares his mother's distress, after his grand father's death.

> "Don't ask Jehangir, he was too young then to understand what was going on."
>
> "I was nine years old, I understood everything."
>
> "Sure. You don't even remember half of it."
>
> "Ask me anything," I challenge him. "I remember exactly what happened." [FM – 495].

This exchange between father and son is representative of the every day quarrels that have become frequent in their house – more between Murad and his father. Yezad has also journeyed from being a person who used to laugh at the religious practices of Coomy to becoming a religious fanatic himself.

(B) Symbol of the Moth

The moth has been used as recurrent symbol in the novels of Rohinton Mistry. It has been used both in the negative as well as the positive aspects. In *Such a Long Journey* we are told how Gustad has covered all the windows with black paper as per the rules of the war. The black paper has lasted through three wars, but he refuses to take them off. His wife at times reminds him to take them off, but he only says that they might be required again. The black paper over the years has acquired layers of dust and cobwebs. Purvi Upadhyay opines,

> At the end of the novel Gustad tears off the black paper covering the ventilators of his flat that had four years "restricted the ingress of all forms of light, earthly and celestial," and a moth, a symbol of past, flies out, a sign of new beginning, a new birth, that emerges from death.[6]

The moth in this text is a symbol of optimism, signaling the beginning of promising things. For a long time, Gustad had refused to take off the black paper from the windows, which is symbolic of his refusing to see the outside world in the proper perspective. This stubbornness on his part gave rise to the deep misunderstanding between him and his son, Sohrab. Sohrab decided to stay away from his father, and was not called back. In the meantime, Gustad goes through a lot of trials, and witnesses the death of three men, who were very close to him – Major Bilimoria, Dinshawji and Tehmul Lungraa. It was at the dead body of Tehmul that he breaks down and welcomes back Sohrab with open arms.

The second novel of Mistry, *A Fine Balance* has the story of Dukhi Mochi and his sons Narayan and Ishvar, who have become tailors from Chamars. Narayan, however, wants to achieve other things in life. After having married and attaining respectability in his village, he questions the government policies. He announces his decision to exercise his voting rights. His father, Dukhi, tries to dissuade him, recounting the way they have attained enough respect in their present position. Narayan merely replies that it was a battle which his father had fought and won. All his father's attempts to make him appreciate the impossibility of the situation fail:

> By and by, she brought a lamp to the porch. Within seconds it attracted a cluster of midges. Then a brown moth arrived to keep its assignation with the light. Dukhi watched it try to beat its fragile wings though the lamp glass. [AFB – 175].

This is Mistry's insertion of a dark omen – preparing readers for great disasters after a lull in the narrative- the moth getting attracted to the light, unknowingly of the death awaiting it. The moth beating its wings in a futile endeavour is symbolic of Narayan's fragile attempts to achieve the impossible, which had to end in disaster. Unlike the earlier novel, where the moth signified optimism, the present one is the opposite signifying pessimism. Narayan goes to vote in the Assembly Elections, is taken captive by Thakur Dharamsi, tortured by his men, hung upside down from a tree and ultimately killed. The Thakur's men later kill the whole family of Narayan – his father, Dukhi, mother, Roopa, wife, Radha and daughters, Leela and Rekha. Only Ishvar and Om who are away in town are spared the horrors which affect their family. Thus the bad women of the moth going towards the light to get killed comes true in the case of Narayan who dared to exercise his rights as an Indian citizen.

In the third novel, *Family Matters*, Mistry again uses his favourite symbol of the moth. Roxana and her family are hard pressed for space and funds after Nariman comes to live with them with a broken ankle. Yezad's salary and Nariman's pension are not sufficient to meet the family's needs. Roxana tries her best to get some help from Coomy and Jal, but they refuse. The money from Nariman's pension is not enough for his medicines. She has to manage from her own household budget. This results in the quality of food gradually going from bad to worse. There is a lot of bitterness in the family as a result of this.

Yezad turns to religion for solace. Coomy conspires to let Nariman not return home before he is finally on his feet. For this, she gets Jal to damage the plaster in Nariman's bedroom, the drawing room and other rooms of the house. When coaxed by Roxana to get the house repaired at the earliest, she agrees to employ Edul Munshi who is ready to work for free. Edul pronounces the beams to be rotten and requiring change. He gets new beams and with the help of two ghatis hoists them on the ceiling. Unfortunately for them the beams come crashing down on Edul and Coomy, killing them instantly.

Some days after the death of Coomy, Jal comes with an idea which will ensure that all of them can stay happily. He suggests that the Chinoy family sell off their flat and shift into the bigger flat at Chateau Felicity. Nariman tries to warn Roxana against this, but she does not understand. He does not want them to go to his flat, as he considers it an unhappy place. But Yezad being out of work for a long time has no choice but agree to Jal's proposal. They make arrangements to sell their flat and move into Chateau Felicity. When they are going away, Jehangir turns in the taxis to have a last look at their flat.

> ... began to move, and Jehangir turned for one last look. Then a moth floated lazily out of the darkened interior of the stairwell. He watched it fly straight towards the bird's open beak. [FM - 445].

According to Bharucha the moth is significant of sinister happenings.

> This dark omen does not bode well for the family and the reader's apprehensions are unfortunately fulfilled as Mistry does not let his unhappy family finally bask in the comfort of a large flat and sufficient money. Instead in the epilogue appended to the novel, he describes their continuing unhappiness five years hence.[7]

Thus the moth is a recurrent symbol in all the novels of Mistry, predicting both happy and sad times.

(C) Motif of Quilt/Jigsaw

In *A Fine Balance*, when Dina's eyesight fails her, she is advised by her friend, Zenobia to approach Mr. Gupta of Au Revoir exports for work. Mrs. Gupta tells her to look for a couple of tailors who would be ready to do piecework for her in her own flat. She finds Ishvar and Omprakash Darji who are as anxious to find work as she is to find tailors. With the tailors stitching, there are several bits and pieces left over which she puts away in her cupboard. She forms an idea that these bits of cloth can be utilized to form a quilt which would be useful for her. Nilufer Bharuch has this opinion of the quilt,

> "Binding their stories of sorrows, troubled times and little joys such as the joint cooking sessions of the tailors with Maneck in Dina's kitchen, is the motif of the quilt that Dina

> makes most evenings. The quilt is a mnemonic device that enables Dina, her tailors and Maneck to recall their lives together. Each remnant, salvaged from the fabric used to make up the Au Revoir orders, has its own particular memory attached to it. Each diverse square, triangle and polygon when sewn together makes a connection with the other pieces to provide a new meaning of its own – 'Just keep connecting patiently, Dinabai – that's the secret. Ji-hahn, it all seems meaningless bits and rags, till you piece it together' (p. 197).[8]

In the chapter entitled 'Return of Solitude' the tailors, Maneck and Dina sit together at night talking about the times spent together. The tailors have decided to go to their village to find a wife for Om. Maneck also would be going away after finishing his course at the college. They discuss the quilt, remembering the occasions when the cloth was brought –

> After dinner Dina resumed work on the quilt. Except for a two-square-foot gap at one end it had grown to the size she wanted, seven by six. ...
>
> "That counterpane looks good, for sure," said Om. 'Should be complete by the time we return.' ...
>
> 'Look Om pointed, 'look at that – the poplin from our first job'.
>
> 'You remember', said Dina, pleased. 'And how fast you finished those first dresses. I though I had found to geniuses.'
>
> 'Hungry stomachs were driving our fingers,' chuckled Ishvar... [AFB – 597, 598].

In this manner the four of them remember all the moments - both happy and sad that they have spent together. This one year has been very valuable for all of them, in which the fact that they hail from diverse backgrounds has not come in the way of their becoming very close, living like a family. And like a close family, they do not want to separate out. They make promises to each other to return soon.

The central motif of *Family Matters* is the Jigsaw that Jehangir always tries to put together. Bharucha feels,

> "much like he tries to puzzle out the quarrels and power politics that rock his family and which he wishes hard would cohere together in happiness and harmony, like the pieces in his jigsaw puzzles. This however is a vain hope as his elders keep falling apart and happiness eludes the family.[9]

The many flashbacks in the novel which have been used in the italic font are a means of Mistry to inform readers of the past life of Nariman. The first flashback can be taken as the first piece of the jigsaw. It tells readers of the time when Nariman's parents had forced him to cut off all relations with the Goan girl, Lucy Braganza, as she did not belong to their Parsi community. They suggest the name of a widow, Yasmin, who has two children.

The second flashback occurs when Nariman is sleeping. He thinks of the time when Lucy decides to work as a domestic servant at the house of the Arjani family who live on the flat below that of the Vakeel's. Nariman is much tortured to see his beloved Lucy working as a domestic help, but is not able to do anything about it.

The third flashback occurs when Nariman has come to stay with the Chinoy family. He sleeps in the drawing room. Jehangir, his grandson, who is nine years old, sleeps beside him on the settee. Jehangir cannot much understand what his grandfather says in his sleep. But he listens very attentively trying to fit the pieces in the Jigsaw puzzle. The third flashback refers to the occasion when Nariman's parents had gone out. He had taken the opportunity to bring home Lucy. Unfortunately, his parents come back very early and discover the two of them in the flat. His father reacts furiously,

> 'This son of mine has turned my house into a *raanwada*, bringing his whore here ! It's the kind of immorality that is destroying the Parsi community [FM - 259].

Nariman is much embarrassed by these comments and replies:

> 'When you call the woman I love a whore, and our home a *raanwada* because I invite her here, you disgrace the role of father. And I despair for you.' [FM - 259].

In the fourth flashback Nariman remembers the time when Lucy and Yasmin were on the rooftop together. He is in a lot of agony because that night had been the cause of the tragedy that his family had faced. Lucy had been in the habit of going up on the roof and singing by herself. She only came down when Nariman asked her to. His wife, Yasmin tried to stop Nariman from going to the roof with Lucy. One night she decides to talk to Lucy herself. Lucy, who has started behaving very differently cannot understand Yasmin's words and does not reply. Yasmin tries to pull Lucy, but both of them fall off the roof to their deaths. Nariman wakes up shouting when he remembers this in his sleep. Jehangir, piece by piece puts the Jigsaw together. He, at last, can make sense of Nariman's talking in sleep.

The Jigsaw puzzle is again mentioned in the Epilogue, when Jehangir reflects thus,

> I go to my room and lie on the bed. I think of all the things I've heard, over the years, about Grandpa and Lucy and my grandmother. And the picture is still not complete. Like some strange jigsaw puzzle of indefinite size. Each time I think it's done, I find a few more pieces. And its form changes again, ever so lightly.

My old jigsaws, including the beautiful Lake Como puzzle, are still on my shelf. ... They seem like a waste of time now. ... There is only one puzzle worth struggling with now. [FM – 490, 491].

(D) Lear Theme

This theme is specific to Mistry's third novel, *Family Matters*. Nariman Vakeel is a professor of English and teaches college students. After the marriage of Roxana, he presents her with a flat at Pleasant Villa. Coomy and Jal, his step children, are very much upset with this action of his. To make them feel at ease, he wills the flat they stay in now, at Chateau Felicity, in their names. For the time being, everything seems to be all right. Things start going wrong when he breaks his ankle in an accidental fall. Coomy and Jal try look after him in bed, but soon grow sick and tired of the entire procedure. Coomy convinces Jal that the best possible way is to let Roxana care for her father. They plan to take Nariman to her flat without prior information. When Nariman is consulted on this, he is non- committal.

> Suppose I say no, thought Nariman, and give Them good reasons- they could still have their way. Suppose I say yes, this flat is my home, and I put it in your names because I did not differentiate between you and Roxana. Would you now throw me out in my helplessness? They would probably that I was getting dramatic. [FM -87]

Nariman feels helpless that the children he trusted so much are now behaving in such an abominable manner. Coomy and Jal take him to their sister's flat and leave him in an uncomfortable state of mind. After some days they conspire to keep him away for a longer time. Coomy gets Jal to damage the roofs and walls of the house and pretend that the water tank overhead had leaked. When Roxana and Yezad go to check for themselves the extent of the damage, Coomy is very rude to them. They come back and report the matter to Nariman, who feels very foolish.

> "To so many classes I taught *Lear*, learning nothing myself. What kind of teacher is that, as foolish at the end of his life as at the beginning?" "What is *Lear*, asked Jehangir. Nariman swallowed the potato. 'It's the name of a king who made many mistskes." [FM -197]

Mistry seems to equate the life of Nariman to Shakespeare's *King Lear*. Nariman meets with the same fate as that of Lear in *King Lear.* The children Nariman trusted so much are unkind to him in his old age. He feels as foolish as Lear must have felt when he was treated badly by Reagan and Goneril. He had put his flat in his step children's names so that they don't feel bad, but they returned his kindness with unkindness. Nilufer Bharucha however argues that Coomy cannot be equated to Lear's unkind daughters as she had made an honest attempt to take care of her step- father, but had to take the extreme step because she was helpless.

(E) Role of Destiny/Chance

Rohinton Mistry's novels seem to resemble those of Thomas Hardy in more ways than one. They are all set in Bombay like Hardy's works in Wessex. Another striking feature common to both writers is the importance attributed to destiny/ chance in their fictional work.

In his view of life, Rohinton Mistry seems to resemble that of Hardy. At first sight their novels present a gloomy view of life. Their faith in determinism makes him a pessimist, who sees no glory in life, little scope for happiness and perfection, man struggling in vain against an unsympathetic nature and adverse circumstances. Their characters seem to snatch at happiness, striving to express and fulfill themselves, but only breaking themselves against a power that takes no heed of them. The historical contemplation of Wessex in the case of Hardy and Bombay in the case of Mistry seem to be partly responsible for this gloomy view. The insignificance of man and the briefness of his life are always present in Hardy's mind.

The lives of Gustad Noble, Dina Dalal, Maneck Kohlah, Dukhi Mochi, Ishvar and Omprakash Darji, Mr. Kapur, Nariman, Yezad, Coomy and Roxana all bear testimony to this fact. They are helpless against the circumstances of life. They, at times, feel powerless against fate. Gustad cannot control Sohrab's not joining IIT, cannot help Roshan to get well quickly even though he would like to. Dina Dalal tries her best to remain independent, but has no control over prevailing circumstances. Her father dies, her mother dies, her husband dies, she still tries to hold her head high. Ultimately, when her eyesight fails, and the tailors don't come back, she is forced to again seek shelter in her brother's house. Nariman wanted to marry Lucy, but married Yasmin instead, thus ruining three lives along with the lives of his step children, Coomy and Jal. Yezad, who does not believe much in religious practices becomes a bigot towards the end of the novel.

It should be noted that Hardy's philosophy of life is marked with a strong sense of fatalism. In Hardy's novels Destiny is character. Man is a helpless creature, a mere puppet at the hands of Destiny or Fate. Man in Hardy's world does not enjoy Free Will. The keen eyes of fate are always looking intently on his activities with a view to intervene as and when it so likes. Man is not free to choose the type of life he wants to live. Obstacles thwart his hopes and aspirations though he continues to wage a futile battle against the odds so created.

Apart from these recurrent motifs and symbols in the novels of Rohinton Mistry there are also instances of humour, irony, celebration of the Parsi idiom in his novels. At times he uses words typical of the Parsi culture and heritage, cuisine, etc. He uses Indian English in a manner which is typical of the characters he represents. At times the narrative shifts back and forth in time, using the technique of flashback as in the case of *Family Matters*. The cover pages of all his novels depict the main theme of the text. On the front cover of *Such a Long Journey,* there are railway tracks symbolic of the various journeys. In *A Fine Balance* there is the picture of a little girl being balanced on a stick which is balanced on the thumb of a man – symbolic of the fine balance between hope and despair, tradition and modernity, life and death, etc. In *Family Matters,* the cover page depicts a Parsi gentleman in a sola topee, with an umbrella in his hand, facing a water body- symbolic of a Parsi custom. Thus Mistry develops the various themes in his novels.

REFERENCES

1. Hariharan, B. 'On the Road: Rohinton Mistry's *Such a Long Journey', South Asian Canadiana,* Eds. Jameela Begum and Maya Dutt, Anu Chitra Publications, Madras, 1996.
2. Nilufer E. Bharucha, *Rohinton Mistry : Ethnic Enclosures and Transcultural Spaces,* Jaipur: Rawat Publications, 2003. p. 120
3. *Ibid.*, p. 134.
4. Purvi N. Upadhyay, " The Journey As Motif and Metaphor in *Such A Long Journey*", Modes of Resistance in Rohinton Mistry's *Such A*

Long Journey, Novy Kapadia, Parsi Fiction Vol. 2, New Delhi: Prestige Books, 2001.

5. Nilufer E. Bharucha, *Rohinton Mistry : Ethnic Enclosures and Transcultural Spaces,* Jaipur: Rawat Publications, 2003.
6. Purvi N. Upadhyay, "The Journey As Motif and Metaphor in *Such A Long Journey*", Modes of Resistance in Rohinton Mistry's *Such A Long Journey,* Novy Kapadia, Parsi Fiction Vol. 2, New Delhi: Prestige Books, 2001.
7. Nilufer E. Bharucha, p. 194.
8. Nilufer E. Bharucha, p. 160.
9. Nilufer E. Bharucha, p. 169.

7

Conclusion

Rohinton Mistry is undoubtedly one of the few Indian fiction writers writing today who have depicted the pathetic condition of the suffering millions. For a person who became a writer by chance, it is a tremendous achievement to have won a prize for all published work.

Rohinton Mistry, born and brought up in Bombay, India, decided to immigrate to Canada, at the age of 23. In Canada he worked as a clerk in a bank and simultaneously took evening classes in Literature and Philosophy. His wife, Freny Elavia, a school teacher also took the classes with him. Mistry became a writer almost by chance. Having won the first prize in the competition, he entered it the following year and again won the first prize.

There after followed a collection of short stories, Tales from Firozshah Baag, his first novel, *Such a Long Journey,* the second novel, *A Fine Balance,* and his third novel, *Family Matters.* It must be mentioned once again that all of Mistry's published work till date have won literary recognition. This is a tremendous achievement for a writer who never intended to become one.

This book, entitled "Critical Insights into the Novels of Rohinton Mistry" is an attempt to analyze the various factors that have contributed to the making of the wonderful writer.

The first chapter, entitled "The World of Rohinton Mistry", looks at the life, work and influences on Rohinton Mistry. It traces his childhood years in Bombay. His family, which consists of his father, mother, two brothers and a sister, lived in a flat, unlike the Parsi Baags that he talks about in detail in almost all of his fictional work. He does not acknowledge any influences on his work. It is left to the readers and critics to find out what could be the possible ones in his life. In his early years in Bombay he was influenced by Bob Dylan, the rock star and imitated his style of singing. His brother, Cyrus Mistry, introduced him to the world of books and also told him that it was not necessary to write about Western settings in order to be a successful writer. He is thankful to his brother for this bit of advice. Almost all his fictional work is set in Bombay, the city of his birth.

The second chapter, entitled Parsiness in Mistry's novels discusses the Parsi elements in the novels of Mistry and the Parsi history from the time the Parsis reached India seeking shelter. It is a well known fact that they agreed to mix with the local population of Gujarat and not proselytize. Mistry like other members of his community is worried about the diminishing number of Parsis in India and the world. His novels record not only the History of the Parsis before their arrival in India, but also faithfully record their rich cultural heritage, customs, religious practices, their Towers of Silence, Cuisine and their idiosyncrasies. Mistry has gone on record to say that after the glorious past of the Parsis, people should remember them by these literary works if not anything else.

In Family Matters, Inspector Masalavala , Jal and Dr. Fitter discuss this very problem.

> "Just before you came, Jal," said Inspector Masalawala, "we were chatting about the future of the Parsi community."...

> "Vultures and crematoriums, both will be redundant," declared Dr. Fitter, "If there are no Parsis to feed them. What's your opinion?"...
>
> "We've been a small community right from the beginning. But we've survived, and prospered."...
>
> "Those were different times, a different world," said Inspector Masalavala, not in a mood to tolerate optimism. "The experts in demographics are confident that fifty years hence, there will be no Parsis left." [FM - 412].

The chapter, Mistry's Bombay Trilogy, traces the use of various Bombay metaphors, 'institutions' as depicted by Mistry in his three novels. In *Such a Long Journey,* Mistry discusses at length the various Bombay landmarks which he remembers prominently. Beginning with the Bhaiya, who supplies milk in the morning, the ubiquitous crow, the Bombay monsoon, Crawford market, Bhindi Bazar, Chor Bazar, Mount Mary Church etc. In *A Fine Balance* Mistry portrays yet another unexplored aspect of Bombay - the lives of the pavement dwellers, the slum dwellers and the middle class life of Bombay. In this novel the period used is that of the Internal Emergency imposed by the then Prime Minister Indira Gandhi. Mistry does not spare the readers any gory details of the life of the beggars. In Family Matters, Bombay as a city is idealized by Mr. Kapur who talks about it as an innocent girl, then a young woman and how the change of name to Mumbai will affect his comfortability. In the novel Inspector Masalawala comments,

> "To think that we Parsis were the ones who built this beautiful city and made it prosper. And in a few more years, there won't be any of us left alive to tell the tale."
>
> "Well, we are dying out, and Bombay is dying as well," said Dr. Fitter. "When the spirit departs, it isn't long before the body decays and disintegrates." [FM-416]

The book also discusses other major themes found in Mistry's novels namely - Matters of the Family and Discordant feminine voices. In *Such a Long Journey,* Mistry through the Family of Gustad Noble depicts the fine relations which make up a Family. For Gustad, there is an extended sense of family which exists in Khodadad Building. Family for him also means relations with close friends like Major Jimmy Bilimoria, Dinshawji and the lame man, Tehmul Langraa. Gustad at times is the only one who bothers about the well being of his friends more than their family does. In *A Fine Balance* Mistry creates a very different sort of family which consist of a Parsi widow, Dina Dalal, her paying guest, Maneck Kohlah and two tailors, Ishvar and Omprakash Darji. Due to strange circumstances, these four people form an unlikely family, sharing each other's joys and sorrows. But as Maneck Kohlah says, 'everything ends badly'. The happy times shared by these people soon come to end. Maneck commits suicide, unable to face life anymore. In the novel Mistry also portrays the family of Monkey man, which consists of a pair of monkeys, named Laila and Majnoo and a dog, Tikka, besides himself. When the monkeys are killed by the dog, Monkey man kills the dog as a just retribution. In the third novel by Mistry, *Family Matters* , readers are brought face to face with a different family setup. Nariman Vakeel, a seventy nine year old, Parsi widower, stays with his two step-children, Coomy and Jal. He also has a daughter, Roxana, who lives with her husband and two sons in a small flat gifted to them by Nariman. Nariman after meeting with an accident, is unceremoniously dumped in Roxana's tiny flat by Coomy and Jal. The readers are then treated to the delicate family relationships that already exist and further deepen between the grandfather and his two grandsons, Murad and Jehangir. Mistry seems to be making a very strong comment on the shabby way old people are treated by their families. Critics claim this book to be Mistry's most mature one. Bharucha feels that Mistry should stick to writing about family relations more than political ones.

The last theme dealt with in this book refers to the Discordant feminine voices in the novels of Mistry. It has been found through a close analysis that the female characters in Mistry's novels do not really come across as round characters. Mistry does not allow them to develop much. Rather they are cast as stereotypes. Dilnavaz, Dina, Roxana, are all beautiful women who are really concerned about their families. They are at times ready to sacrifice whatever they can in order to maintain peace in the family. Bharucha feels that the character of Daisy in *Family Matters* is the most promising one of all the women in Mistry's novels. She is the only one who has achieved much in her career without the support of a man which is quite commendable. She has got the spirit to carry forward, to achieve higher goals.

It has been found that Mistry's novels border on the pessimistic mode, much like that of Thomas Hardy. It should be noted that Hardy's philosophy of life is marked with a strong note of fatalism. In Hardy's novels Destiny is character. Man is a helpless creature, a mere puppet at the hands of Destiny or Fate. Man in Hardy's world does not enjoy Free Will. The keen eyes of fate are always looking intently on his activities with a view to intervene as and when it so likes. Man is not free to choose the type of life he wants to live. Obstacles and hindrances swarm on his path of life, and when it so likes. and they thwart all his hopes and aspirations, though man wages a futile battle against the odds so created.

Nothing is forgotten; slight incidents which are barely noticed at the time, reap later as controlling forces of destiny. As human life is full of tortures, where happiness is but an occasional episode in the general drama of pain, death should be welcome, as being an end to all afflictions. Man should greet death with open arms as if frees him from the bondage of all earthly trials and tribulations.

A struggle between man on the one hand and, on the other an omnipotent and indifferent fate – that is Hardy's interpretation of the human situation. This struggle determines the character and nature of his drama. Like other dramas, this turns on a conflict, but the conflict is not, as in most novels between one man and another, or between man and an institution. Man in Hardy's novels is ranged against impersonal forces, the forces conditioning his fate. Not that his characters themselves are always aware of this. Henchard is obsessed by his hatred of Farfrae; Bathsheba looks on Troy as the author of her misfortunes. But from the point of vantage from which Hardy surveys their stories, Bathsheba and Henchard are seen to be under a delusion. For those whom they think their enemies are as much as themselves puppets in the hands of Fate.

In fact Fate, not they, is ultimately responsible for their quarrels and subsequent miseries. Unless they were destined to do so, they would not be in conflict with each other. Not that Hardy refuses to make moral distinctions between his characters. One the contrary, his leading figures divide themselves into instruments for good and for evil. This line between them is determined by their attitude to themselves. All alike are striving for happiness;

This evidently shows that people will gradually develop a feeling of resignation and indifference, because it is useless to fight against Omnipotent Power. But, on the other hand, it is advisable to develop an attitude of resistance against the shocks and bolts of destiny. The development of a mental shell will enable the man to overcome the depression that will enfeeble his faculties to give a brave fight to his averse fate. In fact, Mistry pictures the future generations, not as beautiful and robust like the Hellenic figures, but as people physically weak but mentally strong. Mistry is of the opinion that in future, the idea of mere joy of living will be replaced by a sense of resignation and indifference towards the joys and sorrows that life offers, and that people will not develop a mental outlook that will feel joy at good fortune nor will it be shocked at the unkind blows of destiny.

Savita Goel opines ‘Mistry, in all his works, gives us a glimpse of Parsi culture and faithfully captures its rhythm. He often disrupts his narrative to include words and, expressions from his native language which is typical of an expatriate writer. Straddling multiple cultures, texts and languages, his novels advocate an embrace of plurality and celebrate hybridity, intermingling, the transformation that comes of new and unexpected combinations of human beings, cultures and ideas and reveal his diasporic consciousness.

His concern has been Parsi community living in India. Mistry's being away from India for years together has not blurred his vision about India. This is where he stands out amongst the expatriate writers; he is not myopic in his vision. He is patriotic in his attitude and this is evident in his writings.

His style is praiseworthy, his prose lucid, his content explosive and overall it is narrative and readable. Structurally his writings are sound, standing on strong pillars as provided by the characters he has created.

Mistry has attempted scaling new heights in his literary pursuit and in his venture he has been a roaring success. His creation of Indian characters in the context of Indian background speaks loudly of expatriate Mistry's love for India and Indians.

REFERENCES

1. Nilufer E. Bharucha, *Rohinton Mistry : Ethnic Enclosures and Transcultural Spaces,* Jaipur : Rawat Publications, 2003. p. 196
2. *Ibid.* p. 207
3. Savita Goel, 'A Literary Voyage to India : Rohinton Mistry's *A Fine Balance',* in Jasbir Jain, *Writers of Indian Diaspore : Theory and Practice,* Jaipur : Rawat Publications, 1998, pp. 197-198.

Bibliography

The Works of Rohinton Mistry

Family Matters, Faber and Faber: London, 2002.

A Fine Balance, McCelland & Stewart Inc.: Toronto, 1995, The First International Vintage Edition : New York, 1996.

Such a Long Journey, Faber and Faber: London, 1991, Rupa & Co.: New Delhi, 1991.

Tales from Firozsha Baag, Faber and Faber: London, 1987, Rupa & Co.: New Delhi, 1993.

Interviews with Rohinton Mistry

Bennett, Dirk. 'Soeaking Out', www.artsworld.com/books-film/nesw/rohinton-mistry.

Gibson, Stacey. 'Such a Long Journey', *University of Toronto Magazine,* Summer 2002.

Gokhale, Veena. 'How Memory Lives and Dies', *The Sunday Review, The Times of India,* October 27, 1996.

Hancock, Geoff. 'An Interview with Rohinton Mistry', *Canadian Fiction Magazine* No. 65, 1989.

Janet, Chimonyo. 'A Flovour of India', www.smh.com.au, June 1 2002.

Jussawalla, Adil, 'Writers Aren't Self-Centred', *MIdday,* September 9, 1988.

Lakhani, Ali. 'The Long Journey of Rohinton Mistry', Interview at the Vancouver International Writer's Festival, publication details not available.

Lambert, Angela. 'Touched with Fire', *The Guardian,* April 26, 2002.

McLay, Robert. 'Rohinton Mistry Talks to Robert McLay', *Wasafiri,* No. 23, Spring 1996.

Saraiya, Indu. 'Luck Played a Great Part', *The Independent,* August 4, 1991.

Select Bibliography

Bhabha, Homi K. 'Freedom's Basis in the Indeterminate', *The Identity in Question,* Ed. John Rajchman, Routledge, London, 1995.

——— *The Location of Culture,* Routledge, London, 1994.

——— Ed.*Nation and Narration,*Routledge, London, 1990.

'On the Irremovable Strangeness of Being Different', PMLA 113, 1, January 1998.

'The Vernacular Cosmopolitan', *Voices of the Crossing : The Impact of Britain on Writers from Asia, the Caribbean and Africa,* Eds. D. Ferdinand & Naseem Khan, Serpent's Tail, London, 2000.

Bharucha, Nilufer E. 'Articulating Silences?: Rohinton Mistry's *A Fine Balance', Critical Practice,* Delhi, Vol. V, No. 1, January 1998.

'The Charting of Cultural Territory: Second Generation Postcolonial Indian English Fiction', *The Postmodern Indian Novel in English,* Ed. Viney Kirpal, Allied Publishers, Bombay, 1996.

'From Behind a Fine Veil : A Feminist Reading of Three Parsi Novels', *Margins of Erasure: Purdah in the subcontinental Novel in Engish,* Eds. Jasbir Jain & Amina Amin, Sterling Publishers Private Limited, Delhi, 1995.

'Imagining the Parsi Diaspora: Narratives on the Wings of Fire', *Shifting Continents/Colliding Cultures: Diaspora Writing of the Indian Subcontinent,* Eds. Ralph J. Crane & Radhika Mohanram, Rodopi, Amsterdam, 2000.

'The Parsi Voice in Recent Indian English Fiction : An Assertion of Ethnic Identity', *Indian English Fiction 1980-1990: An Assessment,* Eds. Nilufer E. Bharucha & Vilas Sarang, B.R. Publishers, Delhi, 1994.

'The Parsi Voice in Western Indian Literature and Journalism: 1820-1920', *The parsi Contribution to Western India: The First Hundred Years* Eds. Nawaz Mody, Allied Publishers, Delhi, 1999.

'When Old Tracks are Lost : Rohinton Mistry's Fiction as Diasporic Discourse', *Journal of Commonwealth Literature,* Vol. XXX, No. 2, 1995.

'Why all this Parsiness? : An assertion of Ethno-Religious Identity in Recent Novels Written by Parsis', in *Mapping Cultural Spaces: Postcolonial Indian English Writing,* Ed. Nilufer E. Bharucha & Vrinda Nabar, Vision Books, Delhi, 1998.

Chimonyo, Janet. *Family Matters,* www.smh.com.au, June 6, 2002.

Dev, Amiya. 'Comparative Literature from Below', *Differential Multilogue: Comparative Literature and National Literature,* Ed. Gurbhagat Singh, Ajanta, Delhi, 1991.

Dharan, N. S. 'Ethnic Atrophy Syndrome in Rohinton Mistry's Fiction', *Parsi Fiction,* Eds. Novy Kapadia, J. Dodiya and R. K. Dhawan, Prestige Books, Delhi, 2001.

Dodiya, Jaydipsingh. Ed. *The Fiction of Rohinton Mistry,* Prestige Books : Delhi, 1998.

Goel, Savita. 'Diasporic Consciousness and Sense of Displacement in the Selected Works of Rohinton Mistry', *Parsi Fiction,* Eds. Novy Kapadia, J. Dodiya & R.K. Dhawan, Prestige Books, Delhi, 2001.

Hariharan, B. 'On the Road: Rohinton Mistry's *Such a Long Journey', South Asian Canadiana,* Eds. Jameela Begum and Maya Dutt, Anu Chitra Publications, Madras, 1996.

Jaggi, Maya. 'Candidates for Compassion: Review *Family Matters',* www.chico.mweb.co.za/art/2002, June 14, 2002.

Lawson, Guy. *A Fine Balance, Mcleans,* Canada, 1996.

'Long Journey of Humiliation Pains Mistry', *Times of India,* 4 November 2002.

Meitei, Mani M. 'Modes of Resistance in Rohinton Mistry's *Such a Long Journey', Parsi Fiction,* Eds. Kapadia et al, Prestige Books, Delhi, 2001.

'Rohinton Mistry's *Such a Long Journey* and its Critical Realism', *Fiction of the Nineties,* Eds. Veena Noble Dass & R. K. Dhawan, Prestige Books, New Delhi, 1994.

Mishra, Chandra Charu. 'Two Cupboards: Transcultural Discourse', *Rohinton Mistry's Short Fiction, Parsi Fiction,* Eds. N. Kapadia, et al, Prestige Books, Delhi, 2001.

Mukherjee, Arun P. 'Whose Post-Colonialism and Whose Postmodernism?', *World Literature Written in English,* 30.2, 1990.

Ramachandra, Ragini. 'Rohinton Mistry's *Such a Long Journey:* Some First Impressions', *Literary Criterion,* Vol. XXIX, No. 4, 1994.

Rao, Damodar K. 'Ordinariness of Dreams, Longevity of the Journey: Story, Statement and Allegory in Rohinton Mistry's Such a Long Journey', *Indian Literature Today,* Vol. 1, Ed. R.K. Dhawan, Prestige, New Delhi, 1994.

Rennison, Nick. *Family Matters,* Amazon.com.uk Review.

Tapping, Craig. 'South Asia / N. America: New Dwellings and the Past', *Reworlding : The Literature of the Indian Diaspora,* Ed. Emmanuel S. Nelson, Greenwood Press, New York, 1992.

Williams, David. 'What's in a Name": Changing Boundaries of Identity in *Such a Long Journey* and *The Puppeteer', Postmodernism and Feminism (Canadian Contexts),* Ed. Shirin Kudchedkar, Pencraft India, Delhi, 1995.

Index

E

F

G

T

U

V

W

Y

Z